Step by St
Databases

Alan Dillon

Gill & Macmillan

Gill & Macmillan Ltd
Hume Avenue
Park West
Dublin 12
with associated companies throughout the world
www.gillmacmillan.ie

0 7171 3497 0

Print origination by Replika Press Pvt. Ltd., India

The paper used in this book is made from the wood pulp of
managed forests. For every tree felled, at least one tree is
planted, thereby renewing natural resources.

A catalogue record is available for this book from the British Library.

Table of Contents

The following symbols are used to indicate Chapter Objectives, Database Assignments, sections covering Database Theory, Database Tasks, Tips and Short-cuts, Important Points and Useful Hints.

 Chapter Objectives

 Database Assignment

 Database Theory

 Database Task

 Tips and Short-cuts

 Important Points

 Useful Hints

Preface

The assignments in this book were written specifically for Microsoft Access 2000 but can also be completed using Microsoft Access for Office XP or Microsoft Access 97. It is a 'learning through practice' book with lots of practical assignments for the student. No previous knowledge of databases is needed as the assignments start at a very basic level. The book contains five sections:

Section 1: Beginners Database Assignments
Section 2: Intermediate Database Assignments
Section 3: Advanced Database Assignments
Section 4: Introduction to Relational Database
Section 5: Project Guidelines and Sample Exams

There are eleven practical database assignments, which are graded by level of difficulty. Each assignment introduces new concepts and, with the exception of Assignment One, enables you to consolidate what you have learned in previous assignments.

Students who have no previous database experience should start at Section 1. Students already familiar with Microsoft Access will be able to use this book as an independent study guide and may wish to start at Section 2. However, these students can practise and consolidate existing database skills by completing Section 1.

By completing all of the assignments contained in Sections 1, 2 and 3, you will have covered all the necessary course material required to successfully complete the FETAC Level 2 Database Methods Module. Students who are studying Level 3 Relational Databases or who simply wish to learn about relational databases should also complete section 4 of *Step by Step Databases*.

New versions of Microsoft Access will be introduced over time. Because the assignments in this workbook deal more with the principles of databases than the features of Microsoft Access, I am confident that, except for a few minor inconsistencies, they will also work with future versions of Microsoft Access.

Thanks to my students for giving me the inspiration and the energy to write this book.

Allan Dillon
January 2003

LECTURERS!
SUPPORT MATERIAL

For your support material check our website at:

www.gillmacmillan.ie

Support material is available to lecturers only within a secure area of this website.

Support material for this book consists of solutions to assignments or tasks.

To access support material for *Step by Step Databases:*

1. Go to www.gillmacmillan.ie
2. Click on the 'logon' button and enter your username and password.
   (If you do not already have a username and password you must register. To do this click the 'register' button and complete the online registration form. Your username and password will then be sent to you by email.)
3. Click on the link 'Support Material'.
4. Select the title *Step by Step Databases.*

Introduction

What is a database?

We all use databases in everyday life, sometimes without even being aware of it. The most common example of a database is the Telephone Directory. Other common examples of databases include Shopping Catalogues, and Brochures providing information on Self-Catering and Bed and Breakfast accommodation. What these three examples have in common is that they all store data in a particular order and that the stored data is divided into sections: for example, in the Telephone Directory the data is divided into three sections – name, address and telephone number, and the stored data is in alphabetical order of name, as shown in Table 0.1.

Table 0.1

Each entry in the telephone
directory has 3 sections

Name	Address	Phone Number
Dunne, Adam	27 Killiney Towers	2682931
Dunne, Aileen	7 Park Drive	2076878
Dunne, Alan	32 Mount Anville Grove	2271883

↑
Data in the telephone
directory is in ascending
alphabetical order of name

So, a database allows us to store data

* in a structured format
* in a particular order.

A database can be recorded on paper or stored in a computer. The examples given are of databases recorded on paper. One of the disadvantages of paper-based databases is that it is time-consuming and cumbersome to find specific data and to view the data in different ways. Imagine trying to compile a list of all the people who live in Dublin 4 from the Telephone Directory! You would firstly have to look through every address and make a note of Dublin 4 addresses. Then you would have to write out the name, address and telephone number of people with a Dublin 4 address in a new list.

What is the advantage of creating a database on computer?

Computerised databases give you great flexibility in the way you view data and also allow you to find specific data in a matter of seconds. Data can be sorted into different orders (in ascending or descending alphabetical order and also in ascending or descending numerical order).

The main differences between a database recorded on paper and a computerised database can be summarised as follows:

Table 0.2

	Database recorded on paper	Computerised Database
Data in a structured format	√	√
Data in a particular order	√	√
Find specific data quickly		√
View data in different orders		√

From Table 0.2, it can be seen that computerised databases offer greater flexibility than databases stored on paper.

This book introduces the learner to computerised databases using Microsoft Access. The learner will be guided through a series of graded assignments. Each assignment introduces new concepts and tasks while building on concepts and tasks learned in previous assignments. For the remainder of the book, the term database is used when referring to a computerised database.

What can a database do for you?

If, in the course of your work, you need to keep track of large amounts of data, and that data is constantly changing or being updated, then a database will save time and reduce errors. For example, a school principal could use a database to store information about students and subjects. This database could produce reports on what students are currently in the college and what subjects they are studying. This information can be used by the school principal when making decisions such as: how many teachers should be employed, how many classrooms are needed and how many exam scripts are required for each subject.

Mail Merge is an important feature of a database. It is used by direct mail and marketing companies to create customised letters for customers stored in a database. The letters are sent to customers to promote products and services of the companies.

Companies, such as the National Car Testing Service, would find it very difficult to keep track of all the data they need to process without the help of a database. Using a database, NCTS can determine which vehicles are due to be tested in the next month. The database generates customised test notifications, which inform each vehicle owner of the test.

In the course of business, people make decisions. The quality of the decision depends on the information on which the decision is based. Business decisions based on accurate database reports, which are available at the click of a button, will be better decisions.

An important point to note is that the database is only as good as the information it stores. If you don't update the database by entering new data as it occurs, the reports produced by the database will be inaccurate.

Structure of a database

A database contains objects. There are seven different types of objects that can be used in an Access database. These are Tables, Queries, Forms, Reports, Pages, Macros and Modules. Each object carries out a different function within the database and should be given a unique name. The database itself must also have a name. A database must have, at the very least, a table to enable it to store data. The number of objects in a database depends on the complexity of the database. More complex databases will have more objects.

Figure 0.1

Creating a database

Before you can create objects such as tables and forms, you must create a database to store the objects. The database is like a container. Initially it is empty but as you work through the assignments you will add tables, queries, forms and reports to each database you create. It is important to note that you must name your database before you start adding objects to it.

The way in which a database is named differs from other popular applications such as word processing and spreadsheets. You can create a new word processing document and start working on it before you save it. You may have two or three pages of typed text before you click the save button.

Access, on the other hand, will not allow you to work with your database unless you give it a name. If you forget to name your database, Access names it for you! (*Normally Access will assign the name* **db1** *to your database.*)

I will use an example of a Tennis Club database to explain each of the seven objects. To keep things simple, the club has only six members. Shown in Figure 0.2 is a new database, named tennis club, which has just been created. At this stage there are no tables, queries, forms, reports, pages, macros or modules in the database.

Figure 0.2

1.  ## ⊞ Tables

Figure 0.3

The table is the most important object in the database. The function of the table is to store data. Data stored in the table must be broken up into smaller pieces of data, known as fields.

Table 0.3

Data stored in the table is divided into sections, known as fields. The field names are in the top row of the table

Member No	Firstname	Surname	Gender	Phone	Date of Birth
1	Paul	Moore	Male	2036558	20/06/1982
2	Deirdre	O Connell	Female	5440291	15/10/1988
3	Seamus	Horgan	Male	8795412	03/01/1987
4	Ross	Mooney	Male	4590298	28/02/1986
5	Cathy	Duffy	Female	8701593	21/08/1985
6	Geraldine	Abbey	Female	3390217	12/12/1989

All the information relating to one member is called a record

2.  ## ⊞ Queries

Figure 0.4

A query allows us to display specific records from the table by asking a question. For example, a query could find all records of female club members.

Table *stores all records*

Table 0.4

Member No	Firstname	Surname	Gender	Phone	Date of Birth
1	Paul	Moore	Male	2036558	20/06/1982
2	Deirdre	O Connell	Female	5440291	15/10/1988
3	Seamus	Horgan	Male	8795412	03/01/1987
4	Ross	Mooney	Male	4590298	28/02/1986
5	Cathy	Duffy	Female	8701593	21/08/1985
6	Geraldine	Abbey	Female	3390217	12/12/1989

Query: *displays some of the records stored in the table in response to a question, in this case female club members*

Table 0.5

Member No	Firstname	Surname	Gender	Phone	Date of Birth
2	Deirdre	O Connell	Female	5440291	15/10/1988
5	Cathy	Duffy	Female	8701593	21/08/1985
6	Geraldine	Abbey	Female	3390217	12/12/1989

3. ▤ Forms

Figure 0.5

The main function of a form is to allow us to enter data into the table. We can also edit or add to data already stored in the table using a form. The form is linked to the table. When you enter data in the form, it filters down into the table.

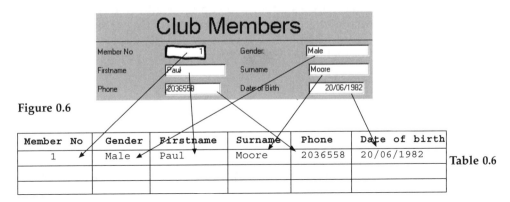

Figure 0.6

Member No	Gender	Firstname	Surname	Phone	Date of birth
1	Male	Paul	Moore	2036558	20/06/1982

Table 0.6

4. ▤ Reports

Figure 0.7

People in business base their decisions on data they receive while they are at work. This data can come from lots of different sources such as business transactions, news reports and colleagues. Often this data has to be summarised and given a particular layout before it can be used as a basis for decision-making. The reporting facility enables us to summarise, format and present data in a way that is easy to understand. In the Tennis Club database, we could use a report to create a Member Contact List as shown in Figure 0.8:

```
Member Contact List

Firstname       Surname        Phone

Cathy           Duffy          8701593

Deirdre         O Connell      5440291

Geraldine       Abbey          3390217

Paul            Moore          2036558

Ross            Mooney         4590298

Seamus          Horgan         8795412

        Number of Members        6
```

Data from a table or query can be formatted and displayed in a report

Report functions can be used to perform calculations on the data displayed in the report

Figure 0.8

5.

Figure 0.9

Pages, or data access pages, allow you to enter and edit data in a database from a web site. Using a data access page, you can view and update data stored in your database from anywhere in the world by connecting to the Internet.

Note: Pages are not included in Microsoft Access 97.

6. ⧉ Macros

Figure 0.10

A macro is a mini computer program. It consists of a series of commands which are carried out in quick succession when the macro is executed. Macros are often used to create custom database menu screens, as shown in Figure 0.11.

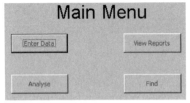

Each button on the form is linked to a macro. Clicking a button runs the macro

Figure 0.11

7. ⧉ Modules

Figure 0.12

A module is a computer program written in Access Visual Basic. Modules can be created to carry out complex tasks such as error checking and data processing.

A database doesn't need to have all seven objects to function efficiently. Pages and modules are more advanced and are not covered in this book.

In this book, you will create databases which have a table and a form, as well as a number of queries and reports. In the Introduction to Relational Database, you will create a more complex database with multiple tables and forms as well as queries and reports. In this section you will also use macros to create custom menus.

Regardless of how complex a particular database assignment is, the first four steps will always be as follows:

1. Create and name the database.
2. Create a table to store the data.
3. Create a form to enter the data.
4. Enter data using the form.

Using database objects

There are two ways that you can view an object.

Figure 0.13

Firstly, you can open an object. Use this option when you want to use the object for a particular purpose. For example, opening a form allows you to enter and edit data. Opening a report displays the data contained in the report. Opening a query displays the records found by that query.

Figure 0.14

Secondly, you can look at how an object is designed. Use this option if you want to change the way in which a table, query, form, report or macro is designed.

Wizards

With the exception of macros and modules, each time you create a new object you have the option of either

1. getting help from a wizard (a help feature in Access)
2. doing all the work yourself by creating the object in design view.

Most of the wizards in Access are very good and can save you a lot of time by doing the basic set-up of an object for you, giving you more time to work on the finer detail. However, some of the wizards are a little confusing, particularly for new database users. As you work through the assignments in this workbook, you will learn how to create objects. Each time you are required to create an object I will recommend whether you should get help from a wizard or create the object in design view.

How do I start using Access?

To start Access double click the Access icon on the desktop.

Figure 0.15

Alternatively click the start button, select programs or all programs and then select Microsoft Access.

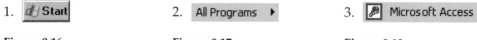

1. Start   2. All Programs ▶   3. Microsoft Access

Figure 0.16   **Figure 0.17**   **Figure 0.18**

How it all works together

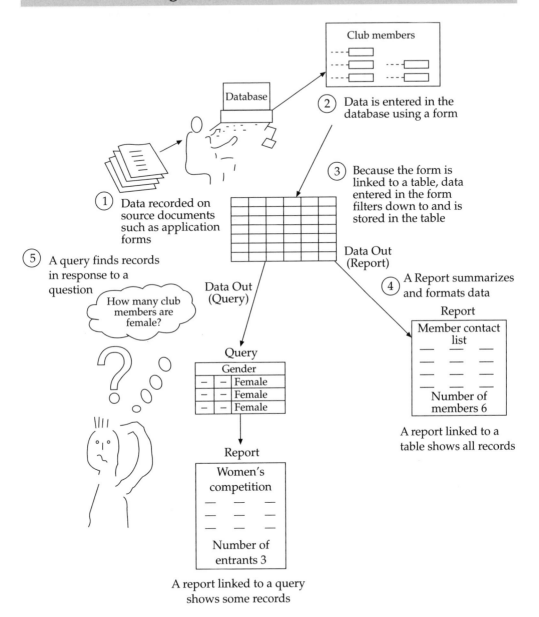

Club members

Database

② Data is entered in the database using a form

① Data recorded on source documents such as application forms

③ Because the form is linked to a table, data entered in the form filters down to and is stored in the table

⑤ A query finds records in response to a question

How many club members are female?

Data Out (Query)

Data Out (Report)

④ A Report summarizes and formats data

Report

Member contact list

Number of members 6

A report linked to a table shows all records

Query

		Gender
–	–	Female
–	–	Female
–	–	Female

Report

Women's competition

Number of entrants 3

A report linked to a query shows some records

Note: In a more complicated database this diagram would have more objects linked together. This will be introduced in the section on Relational Databases.

SECTION 1

Beginners Database Assignments

Assignment One

College of E-Commerce database

Learning objectives

- Create a database
- Create a table to store data
- Create a form to enter data
- Enter data using a form
- Use a form to find a record
- Use a form to edit a record
- Use a form to delete a record

Assignment Two

Pizza Perfection database

Learning objectives

- Create a primary key
- Reposition labels and text boxes on a form
- Add a title to a form
- Find specific records using a query

Assignment Three

Riverside Rugby Club database

Learning objectives

- Use logical operators in query conditions
- Create queries with two conditions
- Define database structure

Assignment Four

Distance Learning database

Learning objectives

- Practise skills learned in Assignment One, Assignment Two and Assignment Three

Assignment One

College of E-Commerce database

Scenario

The College of E-Commerce runs night-classes in a number of different subjects ranging from administration to web design. In Assignment One you will create a database to store and update data relating to students currently attending the college.

College of E-Commerce database

By completing this assignment, you will learn how to

- create a database
- create a table to store data
- create a form to enter data
- enter data using a form
- use a form to find a record
- use a form to edit a record
- use a form to delete a record.

Creating a new database

Figure 1.1

1. To start Access double click the Access icon on the desktop, as shown in Figure 1.1. Alternatively, click the start button, select programs or all programs and then select Microsoft Access.
2. Create a new database by clicking blank access database followed by OK, as shown in Figure 1.2 on page 4.
3. An Access database must be given a name before you can work with it.

Enter the name of the database, in this case **College of E-Commerce**, in the file name box, select $3^1/_2$ floppy (A:) or local disk (C:) in the save in box and then click create, as shown in Figure 1.3 on page 4.

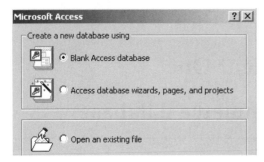

Figure 1.2

Figure 1.3

Your new database is displayed in the database window, as shown in Figure 1.4.

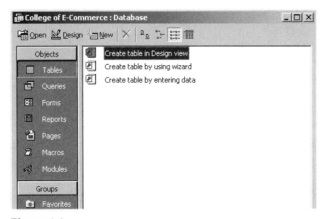

Figure 1.4

The database window lists all the objects in a database. The College of E-Commerce database doesn't have any objects yet. The first object to add to the database is a table. The table will store data relating to students attending the College of E-Commerce.

Tip: Remember to name your database when you create it. If you forget to enter a name for your new database, Access will name it db1.mdb. If you want to open this database at a later stage, you may not remember the name that Access gave it.

Tables

Tables are the most important part of any database. The table stores data. A database must have, at the very least, a table. Before we can store data in a table, we must organise the data so that each record has the same structure. Table 1.1 shows the data that we are going to store in the table. In order to store data in a table, it must be divided into sections, which are called fields.

Table 1.1

Student Code	Student Name	Age	Course	Date Started	Teacher
BS001	Peter Dunne	18	Admin	02/09/2003	Tadhg Allen
BS002	Mark Connolly	17	Admin	02/09/2003	Tadhg Allen
BS003	Dave O Neill	21	Finance	02/09/2003	Gerry Browne
BS004	Maura Keegan	18	Finance	02/09/2003	Gerry Browne
BS005	Ann Murphy	20	Admin	02/09/2003	Tadhg Allen
CP001	Enda Doyle	19	Web Design	09/09/2003	Noelle Duffy
CP002	Seamus Lowry	18	Database	09/09/2003	Liam Kearney
CP003	Jennifer Hayes	18	Database	09/09/2003	Liam Kearney
CP004	Christine O Donnell	20	Web Design	09/09/2003	Noelle Duffy
CP005	Martin Murray	19	Database	09/09/2003	Liam Kearney

All the information relating to one person is called a Record.

The data is divided into 6 columns, each of which is called a FIELD

Creating a table

We will now create a table to store the following data:

Table 1.2

Student Code	Student Name	Age	Course	Date Started	Teacher
BS001	Peter Dunne	18	Admin	02/09/2003	Tadhg Allen
BS002	Mark Connolly	17	Admin	02/09/2003	Tadhg Allen
BS003	Dave O Neill	21	Finance	02/09/2003	Gerry Browne
BS004	Maura Keegan	18	Finance	02/09/2003	Gerry Browne
BS005	Ann Murphy	20	Admin	02/09/2003	Tadhg Allen
CP001	Enda Doyle	19	Web Design	09/09/2003	Noelle Duffy
CP002	Seamus Lowry	18	Database	09/09/2003	Liam Kearney
CP003	Jennifer Hayes	18	Database	09/09/2003	Liam Kearney
CP004	Christine O Donnell	20	Web Design	09/09/2003	Noelle Duffy
CP005	Martin Murray	19	Database	09/09/2003	Liam Kearney

Access gives you three ways to create a table:

1. Create table in design view.
2. Create table by using the wizard.
3. Create table by entering data.

I recommend creating the table in design view. By going through the process of setting up the table design, you will learn, through practice, the principles underlying table design. I don't recommend using the wizard because it is quite confusing, particularly for new database users. Creating the table by entering data is not recommended because Access will not always set up the fields correctly and you will also have to edit the field names once they have been created.

 Create a new table either by double clicking create table in design view or by clicking Tables, New and then selecting Design View. A new table design window is displayed, as shown in Figure 1.5 on page 7.

At the moment the table design is empty. By the time you have finished this section, the table design will contain references to Student Code, Student Name, Age, Course, Date Started and Teacher.

The data displayed in Table 1.2 is divided into six sections (Student Code, Student Name, Age, Course, Date Started and Teacher). Each section is called a

Figure 1.5

field and must be specified in the table design window. A field is created by entering the field name in the table design window. A data type must be specified for each field created. In the case of fields with a data type of text, the field size must also be specified. In Figure 1.6, student code has been entered as the first field name, the data type has been set to text and the field size has been set to 5.

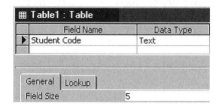

Figure 1.6

Setting a field's data type

There are many different field types that we can use but for the moment, to simplify things, we will use the following rules:

Rule 1: Any field that stores text entries will have a data type of text.
Rule 2: Any field that stores dates will have a data type of date/time.
Rule 3: Any field that stores numbers will have a data type of number.

Setting the field size

This only applies to text fields. Setting the field size for a text field requires the following steps (we will use the student name field as an example):

a. Find the longest entry in the field (in this case Christine O Donnell).
b. Count the number of characters and spaces in this field entry (in this case 19).
c. Enter this number as the field size.

Enter the field names and set the data types and field sizes for all the fields in the table. The resulting table design window should look like the following:

Figure 1.7

  ← Save button

Figure 1.8

Click the Save button to name and save the table. Type **Student Details** in the save as dialog box. Access now asks you if you want to create a primary key. We will use primary keys in Assignment Two. For the moment, click no and then close the table.

The College of E-Commerce database now has one table, which is called student details.

Complete the following table by writing down the longest field entry in the course and teacher fields as well as the number of characters, including spaces:

Table 1.3

Field Name	Longest Field Entry	Number of Characters
Student Code	all entries are the same length	5
Student Name	Christine O Donnell	19
Course		
Teacher		

Check the design of the student details table and ensure that the field sizes of the student code, student name, course and teacher fields match the numbers entered in Table 1.3 above.

Tip: When you are setting up your own database, set the field size of text fields to accommodate existing data and data that will be entered in the future. In this case you will have to guess what the longest entry in a particular text field is likely to be. Setting the field size too low can cause problems later on. For example, if at a later date you tried to enter Geraldine O Callaghan in the student name field, Access would only allow you to enter Geraldine O Callagh. The last two letters are not allowed because that would exceed the field size of 19.

Forms

The main purpose of a form is to enter data in the table. The form can also be used to edit data stored in the table. Forms can make data entry quicker and more accurate through the use of combo boxes, list boxes and other controls, which we will cover from Assignment Four onwards. Forms can also be formatted using colours, fonts and graphics, which can make them more attractive and easy to use. In general, once the table has been set up, you will no longer work with it directly. In order to enter data in the table, we will set up a form that is linked to the table. Each record entered in the form filters down into the table that the form is linked to. So, any data entered in the form will appear in the table. The data is only entered once.

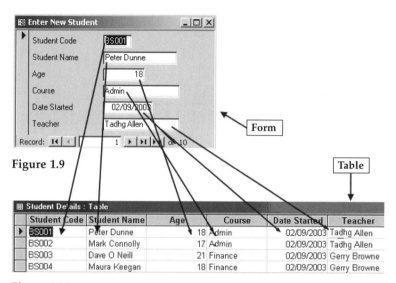

Figure 1.9

Figure 1.10

Creating a form

1. In the database window, click forms and then double click create form by using wizard. Alternatively, click new and then select Form Wizard from the list in Figure 1.11 on page 10.
2. To link the form to the Student Details table, select Student Details from the combo box which appears just above OK and cancel, and then click OK.
3. Click the double arrow (Figure 1.12) to add all the fields in the Student Details table to the form and then click the Next button.
4. Select Columnar as the form layout and then click Next.
5. Select Standard as the Form Style and then click Next.
6. Type **Enter New Student** as the Form Title and then click Finish.
Figure 1.13 shows how the form looks now.

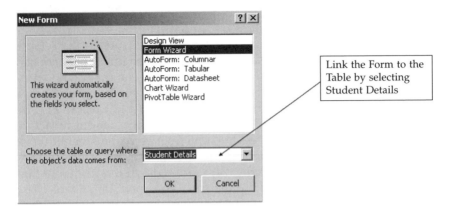

Figure 1.11

Figure 1.12

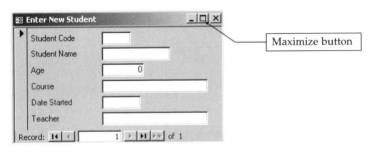

Figure 1.13

There are three ways of viewing a form:

1.  ≣ Form View

   Figure 1.14

   Use this view to enter and edit data using the form. The enter new student form displayed in Figure 1.13 is currently in form view.

2.  ☒ Design View

   Figure 1.15

   Use this view to change the design of your form.

3.  ⊞ Datasheet View

   Figure 1.16

   Use the view to see the data that the form has entered in the table, in row and column format. Datasheet view is more relevant to relational databases where a form can be used to enter data in more than one table.

Click the maximize button and enter all the records, shown in Table 1.4, using the enter new student form. To move to the next field, press the tab key on the keyboard.

Table 1.4

Student Code	Student Name	Age	Course	Date Started	Teacher
BS001	Peter Dunne	18	Admin	02/09/2003	Tadhg Allen
BS002	Mark Connolly	17	Admin	02/09/2003	Tadhg Allen
BS003	Dave O Neill	21	Finance	02/09/2003	Gerry Browne
BS004	Maura Keegan	18	Finance	02/09/2003	Gerry Browne
BS005	Ann Murphy	20	Admin	02/09/2003	Tadhg Allen
CP001	Enda Doyle	19	Web Design	09/09/2003	Noelle Duffy
CP002	Seamus Lowry	18	Database	09/09/2003	Liam Kearney
CP003	Jennifer Hayes	18	Database	09/09/2003	Liam Kearney
CP004	Christine O Donnell	20	Web Design	09/09/2003	Noelle Duffy
CP005	Martin Murray	19	Database	09/09/2003	Liam Kearney

Note: Data is saved automatically as it is entered in a form. There is no need to click the save button to save the records you have entered. You only need to click the save button when you make adjustments to the design of a form.

Adjusting text boxes in a form

Each field in the form consists of a label and a text box (Figure 1.17). The text box for student name is not wide enough to display the text 'Christine O Donnell' and must be widened so that all the data can be displayed.

1. Click the design view button (Figure 1.18). The design of the Enter New Student form appears, as shown in Figure 1.19.
2. Widen the working area of the form.
3. Click the Student Name text box to select it (the text box will have eight dots or 'handles' around it, as shown in Figure 1.20).
4. Widen the student name text box so that it can display 'Christine O Donnell'.
5. In the same way, adjust the width of the other text boxes in the form, if necessary.
6. Click the form view button to view the records in the form. Check that the text

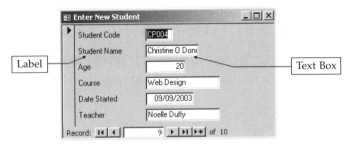

Figure 1.17

Figure 1.18

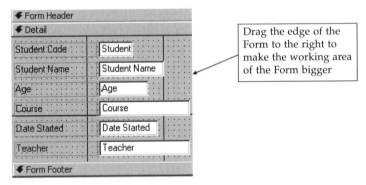

Figure 1.19

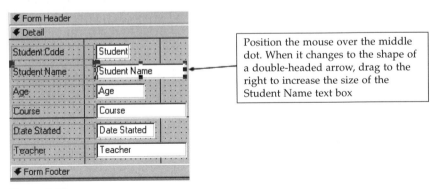

Figure 1.20

Figure 1.21

boxes in the form are wide enough to display all field entries by scrolling through all of the records.

Tip: If you have a wheel-mouse, you can scroll through records by rolling the wheel with your finger.

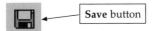

Figure 1.22

7. Click the save button to save the form.

Using a form to find and edit records

Maura Keegan has switched from the finance course to the web design course. This information needs to be updated in the database.

1. With the Enter New Student form open, click in the Student Name text box.

Figure 1.23

2. Click the find button on the toolbar.
3. Type Maura Keegan in the find what box.
4. Click Find Next. Maura Keegan's record is now displayed on the screen.
5. Click in the Course text box and replace Finance with Web Design.

Edit the following records using the Enter New Student form:

- Ann Murphy started on 16/9/2003.
- Martin Murray's age is 20.

Tip: Always click in the appropriate text box before clicking the Find button. For example, if you are searching for a particular student, click in the Student Name text box before clicking the Find button. If you forget to select the appropriate text box, Access will not find the record.

Using a form to delete a record

Figure 1.24

1. Find the record for Mark Connolly using the Find button.

Figure 1.25

2. Click the Delete Record button on the toolbar.
3. Click Yes to confirm that you want to delete the record.

Using a form to add new records

Figure 1.26

Click the New Record button on the toolbar and enter the following information: a new student, Keith Little, aged 19 has joined the Admin course. His start date is 24/09/2003. His teacher will be Tadhg Allen and his student code is BS006.

Toolbar buttons introduced in Assignment One

Figure 1.27

The **Save** button: click this button to save a Table, Query, Form, Report or Macro.

Figure 1.28

The **Design View** button: click this button when you want to change the design of a table, query, form, report or macro.

Figure 1.29

The **Form View** button: click this button when you want to enter data in a form.

Figure 1.30

The **Find** button: while in form view, click this button to search for data stored in a particular field.

Figure 1.31

The **Delete Record** button: click this button to delete the current record displayed in form view.

Figure 1.32

The **New Record** button: in form view, click this button to add a new record to the database.

Assignment Two

Pizza Perfection database

Scenario

Pizza Perfection take orders from customers over the telephone and deliver within the local area. The manager, Gavin Donnelly, is finding it difficult to keep track of orders and amounts owed by customers. Orders are getting mixed up and some customers have been charged the wrong price. In Assignment Two you will create a database to help Gavin manage his pizza delivery business.

Pizza Perfection database

By completing this assignment, you will learn how to
- create a primary key
- reposition labels and text boxes on a form
- add a title to a form
- find specific records using a query.

Task 1   Create a new database named **Pizza Perfection**.

Task 2   Create a table with appropriate field names and data types using the sample data shown in Table 2.1 (*the data type for the total due field is currency*).

Table 2.1

Order Number	Date	Pizza Type	Customer Name	Address	Total Due
1	03/11/2003	Spicy Cheese	Harry O Leary	15 Main Street	€8.95

Save the table as Current Deliveries.   Do not enter data in the table at this point. (*For the moment, do not create a primary key.*)

Primary keys

Every new car that is made is given a unique registration number.

There are a number of reasons for this, such as the need to trace a car if it is stolen or if it was in an accident. Similarly, when you create a database, you will often want to have a way of uniquely identifying each record. If you create a database that stores names, you will run into problems if two people stored in the database have the same name. To get around this problem additional data such as a customer number, test number or order number is often created. In this assignment, an order number is allocated to each pizza ordered. To ensure that we don't use a particular order number more than once, we will identify the Order Number field as being the primary key. Once you do this Access will not allow you to allocate the same order number to more than one record. The second effect of setting Order Number as the primary key is that the table will always be in ascending order of Order Number unless it is sorted in a different order.

 Creating a primary key

1. In design view of the Current Deliveries table, click in the row containing the field that will be identified as the primary key field (the Order Number field).

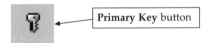

Primary Key button

Figure 2.1

2. Click the primary key button in the toolbar. A key symbol appears next to the Order Number field.

Field Name	Data Type
Order Number	Number
Date	Date/Time
Pizza Type	Text
Customer Name	Text
Address	Text
Total Due	Currency

Current Deliveries : Table

Figure 2.2

3. Click the save button to save the changes.
4. Close the Current Deliveries table.

Task 3 Using the Form Wizard, create a form that includes all fields from the Current Deliveries table, with columnar as the form layout and standard as the form style. The form title is Enter Delivery Details.

 Structure of a form

The form, as it appears on the screen, can be divided into three sections: the Form Header, the Detail Section and the Form Footer.

The form header

This can contain some or all of the following:

- the form title
- graphics, such as a company logo
- instructions on how to use the form
- command buttons that run macros
- database formulas and/or functions.

The detail section

This is the main section of the form. It normally contains all the fields that are included in the form. The detail section is used for data entry and is the most important section of the form.

The form footer

This can contain some or all of the following:

- the date and time
- graphics, such as a company logo
- instructions on how to use the form
- command buttons that run macros
- database formulas and/or functions.

Working in design view of a form

As you work through the assignments in this book, you will learn how to edit and improve the design of a form. When you are working in form design, the appearance of the mouse pointer determines what will happen when you click and drag with the mouse. A summary of the most important mouse pointers is displayed in Table 2.2 on page 19.

Adding a title to a form

When you create a form using the form wizard, it will only have a detail section. The form header and footer can be added in form design.

1. Open the Enter Delivery Details form if it is not already open.
2. If you are not already in design view, click the design view button. Figure 2.8 on page 19 shows what the form should look like.

Table 2.2

Mouse Pointer	Function
Figure 2.3	• Moves a Label and Text Box together as one unit
Figure 2.4	• Moves a Label independently of a Text Box or a Text Box independently of a Label
Figure 2.5	• Increases or decreases the width of a Text Box or Label
Figure 2.6	• Adjusts the height of the Form Header, Detail Section or Form Footer
Figure 2.7	• Adjusts the width of a Form

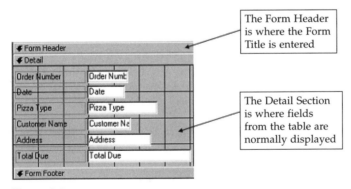

Figure 2.8

3. Open out the form header section of the form and increase the width of the form (Figure 2.9 on page 20).
4. To add a title to the form header, click the Toolbox button (if the toolbox isn't already displayed). Click the Label button and, starting at the top left-hand corner of the form header, drag downwards and to the right to draw a label box that is roughly the size of the form header. Now type the form title as shown in Figure 2.12 on page 20.
5. To centre the form title, select the label and then click the center button. (When the form title is selected, size handles are displayed on the label box as shown in Figure 2.13.)

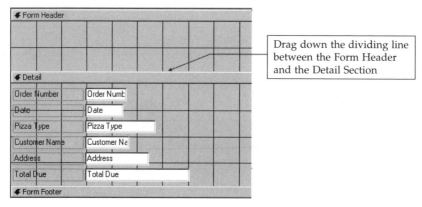

Drag down the dividing line between the Form Header and the Detail Section

Figure 2.9

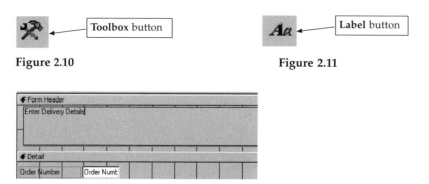

Toolbox button

Figure 2.10

Label button

Figure 2.11

Figure 2.12

Tip: To select the label, firstly click in any part of the detail section of the form. Now point anywhere inside the label and click once.

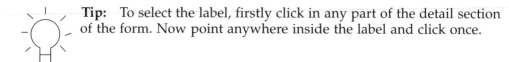

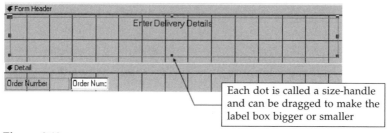

Each dot is called a size-handle and can be dragged to make the label box bigger or smaller

Figure 2.13

Font Size combo box

Figure 2.14

5. Increase the size of the text to 24 using the font size combo box, which is part of the formatting toolbar. The form title now appears as follows:

Figure 2.15

6. Rearrange and resize fields in the detail section of the form as shown in Figure 2.16. To move a field, point at any part of the field, click and hold down the left mouse button and drag to the new location. Adjust the width of text boxes where necessary. (*Some text boxes may be too wide while others may not be wide enough to display all data stored in a field.*) Click the save button to save the changes. The completed form should look like the following:

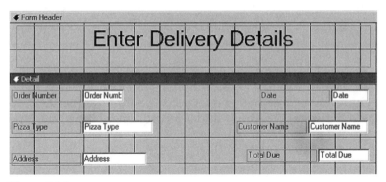

Figure 2.16

Figure 2.17

 Task 4   Click the form view button and enter all the records shown in Table 2.3.

 Tip: There is no need to type the Euro sign. Access does this for you once the data type of the total due field is set to currency.

Table 2.3

Order Number	Date	Pizza Type	Customer Name	Address	Total Due
1	03/11/2003	Spicy Cheese	Harry O Leary	15 Main Street	€8.95
2	03/11/2003	Pesto Pizza	Margaret Kenna	10 Cremore Lawns	€10.50
3	03/11/2003	Mozzarella	Chris Duggan	12 Gledswood Park	€10.00
4	03/11/2003	Ham and Mushroom	Noel Mc Donald	15 Grange Park	€10.95
5	03/11/2003	Vegetarian	Diane O Connor	101 Kings Road	€11.50
6	03/11/2003	Four Seasons	Mary Smith	15 Woodpark	€10.95
7	04/11/2003	Pepperoni	Eamonn Buckley	27 The Pines	€10.50
8	04/11/2003	Vegetarian	John Murphy	5 The Gallops	€11.50
9	04/11/2003	Spicy Cheese	Declan Keane	33 Meadowvale	€8.95
10	04/11/2003	Pepperoni	Emma Daly	Glenview Drive	€10.50

Tip: Always pay close attention to spelling when inputting records. Inputting data incorrectly may cause problems later on when you are searching for specific records with a query. For example, a query set up to find Pepperoni pizzas would not find a record where the pizza type had been incorrectly inputted as *Peperoni*.

Figure 2.18

Figure 2.19

Figure 2.20

Task 5 With the Enter Delivery Details form open, use the Find, Delete record and New Record buttons to make the following changes:

1. Margaret Kenna's order was incorrectly taken and should be a Ham and Mushroom pizza.
2. Diane O Connor's correct address is 103 Kings Road.
3. Declan Keane's order has been cancelled. Delete this record.
4. The following orders have been received and must be entered in the database:

Table 2.4

Order Number	Date	Pizza Type	Customer Name	Address	Total Due
11	04/11/2003	Vegetarian	Mairead Moore	21 Woodpark	€11.50
12	04/11/2003	Spicy Cheese	Liz O Shea	2a Main Street	€8.95

Queries

A query is a very powerful tool which allows database users to find records matching certain conditions. You will often need to find specific records stored in your database. For example, how many customers still owe us money? How many students are registered for the database exam? How many products cost less than €15.00?

We have already seen that you can find a specific record using a form by clicking the find button. This is a useful method if you are looking for one particular record. If, on the other hand, you want to find records which satisfy certain conditions, you should use a query. Usually, when you are creating a query you won't be sure how many records the query will find. Simply tell the query what you are looking for and it will find the records for you.

You tell the query what type of records you are looking for by specifying one or more conditions.

Field:	Order Number	Date	Pizza Type	Customer Name	Address	Total Due
Table:	Current Deliveries	Current Deliveries	Current Deliveries	Current Deliveries	Current Deliveries	Current Deliveries
Sort:						
Show:	☑	☑	☑	☑	☑	☑
Criteria:			"Pepperoni"			
or:						

Figure 2.21

Conditions are entered in the criteria row of the query design grid, as shown in Figure 2.21. In this example, Pepperoni has been entered as the condition for the pizza type field. This query will find all deliveries of Pepperoni pizzas. The result would be as follows:

Table 2.5

Order Number	Date	Pizza Type	Customer Name	Address	Total Due
7	04/11/2003	Pepperoni	Eamonn Buckley	27 The Pines	€10.50
10	04/11/2003	Pepperoni	Emma Daly	Glenview Drive	€10.50

Queries can range from simple (one or two conditions) to extremely complex (multiple conditions). The more conditions you enter in the query design grid, the more specific the search becomes and, in general, the less records will be found by the query. We will start off with simple queries. More complex queries will be introduced in later assignments.

There are two main types of query: select queries and action queries. A query which finds and displays records is called a select query. An action query finds records and then does something with those records. Action queries can be used to delete records, update records and move or copy records from one table to another in a relational database. In Sections 1, 2 and 3 of *Step by Step Databases*, you will learn how to create select queries that search a single table for records. Queries that search for data in multiple tables or in other queries will be introduced in the

Introduction to Relational Database section. Action queries will also be introduced in this section.

How to create a new query

In the following example we will create a query to find deliveries of Vegetarian pizzas, using the design view method.

1. To create a query, select Queries in the database window and then click New. Access presents you with five different methods of creating a query, as shown in Figure 2.22. For the moment we will concentrate on the first two options: design view and simple query wizard. Crosstab queries will be introduced in Assignment Ten. The find duplicates and find unmatched query wizards are beyond the scope of this book.

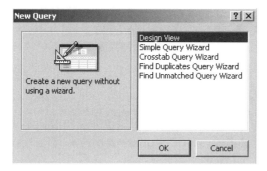

Figure 2.22

Whether you create your queries in design view or by using the simple query wizard, the result will be the same. Which method you use is a matter of personal preference. I find the design view method less confusing.

2. Create the query in design view by selecting Design View and then clicking OK.
3. Click Add to add the Current Deliveries table and then click close.

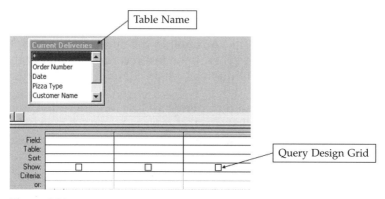

Figure 2.23

4. Before you can enter conditions in the query design grid, the field names must be added to the top row of the grid. This can be done using any one of three methods:

   Method 1: Drag individual fields from the Current Deliveries table and drop them one by one in the query design grid.

   Method 2: Select the fields from a list by clicking in the top row of the query design grid, as shown in Figure 2.24.

Figure 2.24

   Method 3: Double click the table name, drag the highlighted fields and drop in the query design grid.

   Using any one of the three methods, add all the fields from the Current Deliveries table to the query design grid.

5. Type the **query condition** in the **criteria row** of the appropriate field. To find Vegetarian pizzas we must type Vegetarian as the condition for the pizza type field.

Note: Incorrect spelling of the query condition causes errors. For example, if you typed **Vagetarian**, the query would not find any records.

Figure 2.25

6. Click the **Run Button** to see the records found by the query.
7. Click the print button to print the records found by the query (see Figures 2.26 and 2.27 on page 26).
8. Save the query as **Vegetarian Pizzas**. Close the Vegetarian Pizzas query.

Tip: There is no need to type the inverted commas when you are entering the query condition. Access does this for you.

Task 6 Create a new query that finds records of pizzas delivered on 03/11/2003. Save the query as **03/11/2003 deliveries**.

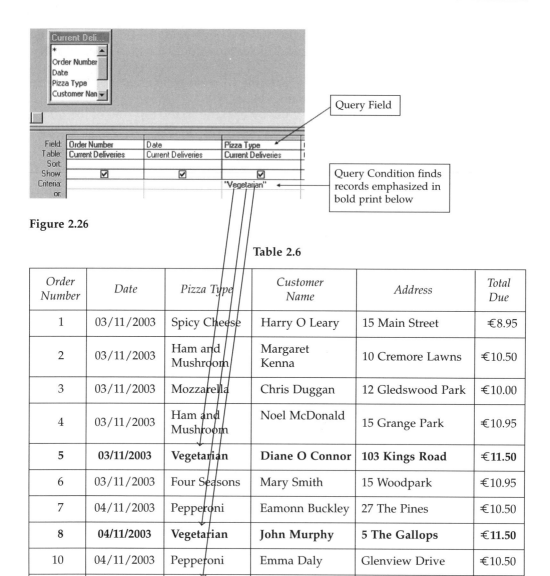

Figure 2.26

Table 2.6

Order Number	Date	Pizza Type	Customer Name	Address	Total Due
1	03/11/2003	Spicy Cheese	Harry O Leary	15 Main Street	€8.95
2	03/11/2003	Ham and Mushroom	Margaret Kenna	10 Cremore Lawns	€10.50
3	03/11/2003	Mozzarella	Chris Duggan	12 Gledswood Park	€10.00
4	03/11/2003	Ham and Mushroom	Noel McDonald	15 Grange Park	€10.95
5	**03/11/2003**	**Vegetarian**	**Diane O Connor**	**103 Kings Road**	**€11.50**
6	03/11/2003	Four Seasons	Mary Smith	15 Woodpark	€10.95
7	04/11/2003	Pepperoni	Eamonn Buckley	27 The Pines	€10.50
8	**04/11/2003**	**Vegetarian**	**John Murphy**	**5 The Gallops**	**€11.50**
10	04/11/2003	Pepperoni	Emma Daly	Glenview Drive	€10.50
11	**04/11/2003**	**Vegetarian**	**Mairead Moore**	**21 Woodpark**	**€11.50**
12	04/11/2003	Spicy Cheese	Liz O Shea	2a Main Street	€8.95

 **Print** button

Figure 2.27

Task 7   Create a new query to find records of deliveries where the total due is €10.50. Save the query as **Deliveries costing ten Euro fifty cents**.

Note: If you type €**10.50** as the query condition, Access displays the message 'data type mismatch in criteria expression'. This is because the Euro symbol(€) is text. The total due field is a currency field which stores numbers. Access will not allow you to enter a query condition containing text for a field which stores numbers.

Tip: Never type the Euro symbol (€) when you are creating a query condition in a currency field.

Toolbar buttons introduced in Assignment Two

Figure 2.28

The **Primary Key** button: in table design, click this button to identify the selected field as the primary key.

Figure 2.29

The **Toolbox** button: click this button to display the toolbox in form design or report design.

Figure 2.30

The **Label** button: to insert text on a form or a report, click the label button and draw a box. The text is then entered in the box.

Figure 2.31

The **Run** button: click this button to see the records that are selected by a query.

Figure 2.32

The **Print** button: click this button to print any object in the database.

Assignment Three

Riverside Rugby Club database

Scenario

Paddy Johnson is coach to Riverside Rugby Club. In order to improve their performance he has been analysing player statistics from recent matches but is finding this very difficult and time consuming. In Assignment Three you will create a database to store and analyse data relating to players and their match performances.

Riverside Rugby Club database

By completing this assignment, you will learn how to

- use logical operators in query conditions
- create a query with two conditions
- define database structure.

More about data types and field sizes

So far we have created fields using text, date and time, currency and number data types. Each data type has a field size associated with it that determines the amount of storage space (measured in bytes) required to store data in a particular field. What we have covered so far may be summarised as follows:

Table 3.1

Data Type	Field Size
Text	Variable – depends on number of characters in the longest field entry
Date and Time	8 Bytes
Currency	8 Bytes
Number	Depends on the type of number selected

Yes/No data type

A yes/no data type should be used where one of two possible data items can be entered in a particular field. These will normally be either 'yes' and 'no', 'true' and 'false' or 'on' and 'off'. The classic example of a field requiring a yes/no data type is a paid field. In a customer database, yes would be entered in the paid field when customers have paid. No would be entered for customers who haven't paid. The field size of a yes/no field is 1 byte.

Byte number type

Up to now I have not specified the different types of numbers which can be used in a table. In this assignment, we will use the first type of number, which is simply called a byte.

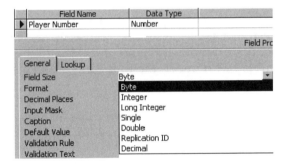

Figure 3.1

Shown in figure 3.1 is the Player Number field, one of the fields to be created in this assignment. The data type of player number field is Number and Byte has been selected as the field size.

Setting the field size of a number to byte has three effects:

1. You will be able to enter whole numbers (no fractions) in that field.
2. You will be able to enter numbers in the range 0–255 inclusive in that field.
3. Data entered in that field will require 1 byte of storage space on disk, per record.

Because player numbers will never be higher than 255 and will not include fractions, the Player Number field is set as number with a field size of byte.

Set the field size of a number to byte if you are sure that:

- you will only enter whole numbers in that field
- you won't be entering negative numbers or numbers greater than 255 in that field.

A good example of this is a field that stores the age of a person. A person's age cannot be a negative number and will never be greater than 255.

 Task 1 Create a new database named **Riverside Rugby Club.**

Task 2 Create a table with appropriate field names and data types using the sample data shown as follows:

Table 3.2

Player Number	Player Name	Position	No of Tackles	No of Passes	No of Errors	Player Rating
1	Darragh Foley	Forward	5	2	3	6

Set the player number field as the primary key. **Save the table as Players**. Do not enter data in the table at this point.

Note: It is important to get your data types correct at this stage. Setting a data type incorrectly in table design can cause errors in queries and reports later on. For example, if the no of tackles field is given a data type of text instead of number, the following problems may occur:

1. Use of the logical operators <, <=, > or >= in queries may produce incorrect results. *For example, <2 could potentially find 0, 1, 10, 11, 12, 13, 14, 15, 16, 17, 18 and 19 in a text field.*
2. Sorting by the no of tackles field will not display data in ascending or descending **numerical** order. Data would be displayed in the following order: *0, 1, 10, 11, 12, 13, 14, 15, 16, 17, 18, 19, 2, 20, 21 etc. where the data type of the no of tackles field is set as text.*

 Task 3 Using the form wizard, create a form that includes all fields from the Players table, with columnar as the form layout and standard as the form style. The form title is **Enter Match Stats**. Add a label box to the form header, reposition labels and text boxes and adjust the width of text boxes where appropriate, as shown in Figure 3.2:

Enter Match Stats

Player Number	0		
Player Name		Position	
No of Tackles	0	No of Passes	0
No of Errors	0	Player Rating	0

Figure 3.2

Tip: To move a label independently of a text box, firstly click the label to select it. Using the mouse, point at the size handle at the top left-hand corner of the label. This size handle is bigger than all the others. When the mouse pointer changes to a pointing hand, click and drag to move the label. A text box can be moved independently of a label, using the same method.

Task 4 Using the Enter Match Stats form, enter all the records shown in Table 3.3.

Table 3.3

Player Number	Player Name	Position	No of Tackles	No of Passes	No of Errors	Player Rating
1	Darragh Foley	Forward	5	2	3	6
2	Shay Lunny	Forward	9	4	4	7
3	Eddy Moran	Forward	6	2	1	6
4	Nick O Kelly	Forward	10	3	2	8
5	Declan Hennesey	Forward	8	1	3	6
6	Sean Hayes	Forward	11	2	1	8
7	Tom Wood	Forward	10	5	1	9
8	Aidan Clohosey	Back	5	2	2	7
9	Mick Moloney	Back	7	40	2	8
10	Gerard Byrne	Back	4	12	4	7
11	Fionn O Sullivan	Centre	4	5	1	10
12	James O Driscoll	Centre	9	2	0	8
13	Ciaran Higgins	Back	3	5	1	8
14	Paul Murray	Back	1	2	1	6
15	Graham Nolan	Back	3	3	0	7

Task 5 With the Enter Match Stats form open, use the Find and New Record buttons to make the following changes:

1. Aidan Clohosey is a forward and not a back as recorded.
2. Tom Wood made 12 tackles.
3. Gerard Byrne made 3 errors.
4. Nick O Kelly's player rating is 7.

5. Brendan Byrne came on as a sub during the match. Enter his details, shown in Table 3.4.

Table 3.4

Player Number	Player Name	Position	No of Tackles	No of Passes	No of Errors	Player Rating
16	Brendan Byrne	Forward	5	0	2	6

Setting field sizes of text fields

To set the field sizes of text fields in the players table, count the number of characters and spaces in the longest entry in each text field and then enter this number as the field size in table design. The reason for this is to minimise the amount of disk space required to store data entered in that field.

In the case of the player name field the longest field entry is 'James O Driscoll', which requires a field size of 16 (*14 letters and 2 spaces*).

Setting the field size of the player name field to 16 means that all data entered in that field will now require 16 bytes of disk storage, regardless of the number of characters and spaces entered in the field. For example, 'Tom Wood' has 8 characters (7 letters and a space), but once this is entered, it will require 16 bytes of storage because the field size of the player name field is 16. Eight bytes of storage are wasted because only 8 of the 16 bytes are used.

Once the field size is set to 16, the player name field will be unable to store more than 16 characters as new records are added. When setting the field size of a text field, there are two important factors to consider:

1. the longest text entry currently stored in that field
2. what data will be entered in that field in the future.

Because the default size for text fields is 50, each time we create a text field, it is given a field size of 50. In the case of the player name field, if we don't change the field size from 50 to 16, then 42 bytes of storage space will be wasted.

Table 3.5

Player name field

8 bytes

Tom Wood	8 bytes wasted space

16 bytes

8 bytes

Tom Wood	42 bytes wasted space

50 bytes

Table 3.5 illustrates the importance of setting the field size of a text field to the number of characters and spaces in the longest field entry.

Using logical operators in a query condition

Logical operators can be used in a query to find records where numbers stored in a particular field are

- less than
- less than or equal to
- equal to
- greater than
- greater than or equal to
- not equal to

a value entered in a query condition.

Logical operators can also be used in a query to find records where numbers in a particular field are

- between two values entered in a query condition.

I will use the no of tackles field, shown in Table 3.6, to explain the effect of using each logical operator as a query condition.

Table 3.6

Player Number	Player Name	No of Tackles
1	Darragh Foley	5
2	Shay Lunny	9
3	Eddy Moran	6
4	Nick O Kelly	10
5	Declan Hennesey	8
6	Sean Hayes	11
7	Tom Wood	12
8	Aidan Clohosey	5
9	Mick Moloney	7
10	Gerard Byrne	4
11	Fionn O Sullivan	4
12	James O Driscoll	9
13	Ciaran Higgins	3
14	Paul Murray	1
15	Graham Nolan	3
16	Brendan Byrne	5

Table 3.7

Logical Operator	Meaning	Example (based on conditions entered in the number of tackles field in the query design grid)	Number of records found
<	Less than	**<5** *finds 4, 4, 3, 1 and 3*	5
<=	Less than or equal to	**<=5** *finds 5, 5, 4, 4, 3, 1, 3 and 5*	8
=	Equal to	**5** *finds 5, 5 and 5*	3
>	Greater than	**>5** *finds 9, 6, 10, 8, 11, 12, 7 and 9*	8
>=	Greater than or equal to	**>=5** *finds 5, 9, 6, 10, 8, 11, 12, 5, 7, 9 and 5*	11
<>	Not equal to	**<>5** *finds 9, 6, 10, 8, 11, 12, 7, 4, 4, 9, 3, 1 and 3*	13
Between	Records within a range including the highest and lowest number	**Between 5 and 8** *finds 5, 6, 8, 5, 7 and 5*	16

Note: The logical operator **not** can be used instead of <>. Entering **not 5** as a condition in the no of tackles field also finds 13 records. Not is widely used in database programming. <> is generally used in queries.

The following examples demonstrate how to use logical operators in a query.

Example 1: (Logical operator used in one field)

Field:	Player Number	Player Name	Position	No of tackles
Table:	Players	Players	Players	Players
Sort:				
Show:	☑	☑	☑	☑
Criteria:				<5
or:				

Figure 3.3

Entering the logical operator in Figure 3.3 finds players who made less than 5 tackles, as shown in Table 3.8.

Table 3.8: *Five records found by entering <5 as a condition in the no of tackles field*

Table 3.8

Player Number	Player Name	Position	No of Tackles	No of Passes	No of Errors	Player Rating
10	Gerard Byrne	Back	4	12	3	7
11	Fionn O Sullivan	Centre	4	5	1	10
13	Ciaran Higgins	Back	3	5	1	8
14	Paul Murray	Back	1	2	1	6
15	Graham Nolan	Back	3	3	0	7

Example 2: (logical operator used in two fields)
In this example, two conditions have been entered in the query design grid, each of which is a logical operator, to find players who made less than 5 tackles and whose rating was greater than 7.

Including more than one condition in a query refines the search and in most cases will result in the query finding fewer records.

Field:	Player Name	Position	No of tackles	No of passes	No of errors	Player Rating
Table:	Players	Players	Players	Players	Players	Players
Sort:						
Show:	☑	☑	☑	☑	☑	☑
Criteria:			<5			>7
or:						

Figure 3.4

Placing the conditions in the same criteria line in the query means that the database will interpret the conditions as being linked. In Figure 3.4, the query finds players who made less than 5 tackles **and** whose rating is greater than 7. Including a second condition in the query has reduced the amount of records found from 5 records to 2 records.

Table 3.9: *Two records found by entering <5 as a condition in the no of tackles field and >7 as a condition in the player rating field*

Table 3.9

Player Number	Player Name	Position	No of Tackles	No of Passes	No of Errors	Player Rating
11	Fionn O Sullivan	Centre	4	5	1	10
13	Ciaran Higgins	Back	3	5	1	8

Example 3: (using Between as a logical operator)
In Example 3, **Between** is used as a logical operator to find players who made between 5 and 8 tackles inclusive.

Field:	Player Number	Player Name	Position	No of tackles	No of passes
Table:	Players	Players	Players	Players	Players
Sort:					
Show:	☑	☑	☑	☑	☑
Criteria:				Between 5 And 8	
or:					

Figure 3.5

Table 3.10 shown on page 36: *Six records found by entering between 5 and 8 as a condition in the no of tackles field*

Create a separate query for each task described in Table 3.11. Save each query using the name provided.

Table 3.10

Player Number	Player Name	Position	No of Tackles	No of Passes	No of Errors	Player Rating
1	Darragh Foley	Forward	5	2	3	6
3	Eddy Moran	Forward	6	2	1	6
5	Declan Hennesey	Forward	8	1	3	6
8	Aidan Clohosey	Forward	5	2	2	7
9	Mick Moloney	Back	7	40	2	8
16	Brendan Byrne	Forward	5	0	2	6

Table 3.11

		Purpose of Query	Query Name
Task 6		Find records of players who made less than 2 errors	Made less than 2 errors
Task 7		Find records of players who made less than 3 passes	Made less than 3 passes
Task 8		Find records of players with a rating of 7 or less	Player rating of 7 or less
Task 9		Find records of players who made 5 tackles	Made 5 tackles
Task 10		Find records of players who made only 1 error	Made 1 error
Task 11		Find records of players who made more than 6 tackles	Made more than 6 tackles
Task 12		Find records of players who made more than 5 passes	Made more than 5 passes
Task 13		Find records of players with a rating of 8 or more	Player rating of 8 or more
Task 14		Find records of players who are not centres	All players excluding centres
Task 15		Find records of players whose rating is between 6 and 8 inclusive	Player rating between 6 and 8
Task 16		Find records of forwards who made 8 or more tackles	Forwards who made 8 or more tackles
Task 17		Find records of backs who made 4 or more tackles	Backs who made 4 or more tackles

Task 18   Create a query to find players who made between 7 and 10 tackles inclusive. Save the query as **made between 7 and 10 tackles**. Print the records found by this query.

 Tip: Preview the query before you print it. If all the data does not fit on a page in portrait orientation, select **File** followed by **Print** and then click the **Properties** button in the Print dialog box. Now click the layout tab and select landscape as the page orientation.

Defining database structure

It is good database practice to keep a record of the structure of your database in a separate word processing document, known as the database structure form. You will need to refer to this document if you are making alterations to the database, if you haven't worked with a particular database for a period of time and need to refresh your memory or if you have been assigned responsibility for a database that was designed by someone else.

In a single table database, we need to specify the field names, field sizes (in bytes) and data types. This information can be found in design view of the Players table as shown in Figure 3.6.

Field Name	Data Type
▶ Player Number	Number

General	Lookup
Field Size	Byte

Figure 3.6

Using this information, we can fill in the first line of the database structure form.

Database structure form

Table 3.12

Field Name	Data Type	Field Size
Player Number	Number	Byte(1)

For number fields, the field size in bytes is not given in table design. When the data type of a field is set to number-byte, this automatically sets the field size to 1. Details of the next field in the table are shown in Figure 3.7. (Remember that for text fields, the field size should be set to the number of characters and spaces in the longest entry in that particular field – in this case James O Driscoll.)

Continuing the example, we can fill in the information relating to the Player Name field as shown in Table 3.13 on page 38.

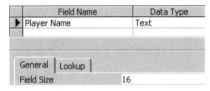

Figure 3.7

Database structure form

Table 3.13

Field Name	Data Type	Field Size
Player Number	Number	Byte(1)
Player Name	Text	16

Task 19 Complete the following database structure form for the remaining fields in the table:

Database structure form

Table 3.14

Field Name	Data Type	Field Size
Player Number	Number	Byte(1)
Player Name	Text	16
Position		
No of Tackles		
No of Passes		
No of Errors		
Player Rating		

Task 20 Ensure that the field sizes of text fields specified in design view of the Players table match those specified in the database structure form.

Assignment Four

Distance Learning database

Scenario

Debbie Riordan is responsible for the organisation of hardware and software provided for students studying by distance learning. She is finding it difficult to keep track of students who have PCs belonging to the college. Recently she couldn't find CDs containing applications software and course work and was unable to determine which student has them at present. In Assignment Four you will create a database to help Debbie manage the allocation of hardware and software to students.

Distance learning database

By completing this assignment, you will

- practise skills learned in Assignment One, Assignment Two and Assignment Three.

Task 1 Create a new database named **Distance Learning**.

Task 2 Create a table with appropriate field names and data types using the sample data shown in Table 4.1. (*The data type for MS Office, ECDL CD and Current is Yes/No.*)

Table 4.1

Student Number	First-Name	Surname	Phone	PC	Email	MS Office	ECDL CD	Current	PC No.
1	Michael	Noonan	2043980	Own	mnoo @esat.net	Yes	Yes	No	1

Set the Student Number field as the primary key. **Save the table as Students**. Do not enter data in the table at this point.

Task 3 Using the form wizard, create a form that includes all fields from the Students table, with columnar as the form layout and standard as the form style. The form title is **Student Information**. Design the form as shown in Figure 4.1. Adjust the width of text boxes where appropriate.

Student Information

Student Number	[1]
Firstname [ ]	Surname [ ]
Phone [ ]	PC [ ]
Email [ ]	MS Office ☐
	ECDL CD ☐
PC No [0]	Current ☐

Figure 4.1

Task 4 Using the Student Information form, enter all the records shown in Table 4.2.

Note: Ticking the MS Office, ECDL CD and current check boxes is equivalent to entering yes in each of these fields, while not ticking them is equivalent to entering no.

Table 4.2

Student Number	First-Name	Surname	Phone	PC	Email	MS Office	ECDL CD	Current	PC No.
1	Michael	Noonan	2043980	Own	mnoo@esat.net	Yes	Yes	No	1
2	Peter	Jones	2881983	Loan	petej@hotmail.com	Yes	No	Yes	22
3	Anne	Ward	8209396	Loan	anne200@yahoo.com	Yes	No	Yes	8
4	Liz	Sheils	4932042	Own	lizsh@Ireland.com	Yes	No	Yes	3
5	Adam	Lacey	2857498	Loan	adlcy@hotmail.com	No	Yes	Yes	15
6	Tony	O Shea	4724161	Loan	tosh@eircom.net	No	Yes	Yes	12
7	Avril	Kearney	8338017	Loan	avrilk@indigo.ie	Yes	Yes	No	10
8	Frank	Donoghue	4554279	Own	fdonoghue@esat.net	No	Yes	Yes	2
9	Denis	Robinson	4992266	Own	drob@yahoo.com	Yes	No	Yes	5

Table 4.2 *(contd)*

Student Number	First-Name	Surname	Phone	PC	Email	MS Office	ECDL CD	Current	PC No.
10	John	Delaney	2993676	Loan	jdl55 @hotmail.com	No	No	Yes	7
11	Susan	Mc Grath	2886134	Loan	smg @gofree.net	Yes	No	Yes	6
12	Hugh	O Keefe	4510501	Own	hok @oceanfree.net	Yes	Yes	Yes	11
13	Brenda	Hickey	4985857	Own	bhickey @eircom.net	Yes	Yes	Yes	20
14	Bernard	Kennedy	8397845	Loan	bkennedy @indigo.ie	No	No	No	21
15	Erica	Sullivan	6264457	Loan	erica @Ireland.com	Yes	No	Yes	13
16	Pamela	Galvin	8333359	Own	pgalvin @yahoo.com	Yes	Yes	Yes	18
17	Fran	Byrne	8944055	Own	fran @oceanfree.net	No	Yes	No	17
18	Daniel	Conroy	2962138	Loan	dconroy @eircom.net	No	No	No	16
19	Valerie	Whelan	8936274	Loan	vwhelan100 @hotmail.com	Yes	No	Yes	19

 Task 5   Complete the following data structure form by entering data types and field sizes for all fields in the Students table:

Table 4.3

Field Name	Data Type	Field Size
Student Number		
Firstname		
Surname		
Phone		
PC		
Email		

Table 4.3 *(Contd)*

Field Name	Data Type	Field Size
MS Office		
ECDL CD		
Current		
PC No		

Ensure that the field sizes of text fields specified in design view of the Students table match those specified in the database structure form.

Task 6 Open the Student Information form and use the Find and New Record buttons to make the following changes:

1. Anne Ward is no longer on the course.
2. Micheal Noonan has not finished the course.
3. John Delaney's email address is jdl54@hotmail.com
4. Hugh O Keefe doesn't have an ECDL CD.
5. Valerie Whelan's phone number is 8836274.
6. A new student has started and his record needs to be added:

Table 4.4

Student Number	First- Name	Surname	Phone	PC	Email	MS Office	ECDL CD	Current	PC No.
20	Ciaran	Murphy	2012339	Own	cmpy @eircom.net	No	No	Yes	4

Create a separate query for each of the tasks described in Table 4.5 on page 43. Save each query using the name provided.

 Task 13 Print the records found by the Location of PCs 1 to 10 query and the Location of PCs 11 to 22 query.

Table 4.5

	Purpose of Query	Query Name
Task 7	Find records of students currently on the course	List of current students
Task 8	Find records of current students who have their own PC	Current students with own PC
Task 9	Find records of students who have finished the course and still have the ECDL CD	ECDL CDs to be returned
Task 10	Find records of current students who need to have MS Office installed on their PCs	MS office installations
Task 11	Find records of students who have PCs 1 to 10	Location of PCs 1 to 10
Task 12	Find records of students who have PCs 11 to 22	Location of PCs 11 to 22

Progress test 1

Complete the test by circling the correct answer for each question.

1. In a database, which object stores data?

    a. Table
    b. Query
    c. Form
    d. Report

2. The highest number that can be entered in a number field, whose field size in bytes is:

    a. 55
    b. 155
    c. 255
    d. 355

3. The logical expressions 'between 1 and 5' will find which of the following sets of numbers?

    a. 2, 3, 4
    b. 1, 2, 3, 4
    c. 2, 3, 4, 5
    d. 1, 2, 3, 4, 5

4. The title of a form is normally entered in the

    a. Page header
    b. Form header
    c. Detail section
    d. Form footer

5. A database cannot function without a

    a. Table
    b. Query

    c. Form
    d. Report

6. Which of the following buttons is used to enter a new record?

    a.

    Figure 4.2

    b.

    Figure 4.3

    c.

    Figure 4.4

    d.  ▣ ▾

    Figure 4.5

7. A query condition should be entered in the

    a. Field row of the query design grid
    b. Sort row of the query design grid
    c. Show row of the query design grid
    d. Criteria row of the query design grid

8. The field size of a currency field is

    a. 1 byte
    b. 2 bytes
    c. 4 bytes
    d. 8 bytes

9. Which of the following logical operators means 'not equal to'?

    a. <>
    b. <=
    c. >
    d. >=

10. Which of the following buttons is used to view the design of an object?

    a.  ▣ ▾

    Figure 4.6

b.

Figure 4.7

c.

Figure 4.8

d.

Figure 4.9

SECTION 2

Intermediate Database Assignments

Assignment Five

National Railways database

Learning objectives

- Create a combo box to enter data in a form
- Change the tab order in a form
- Create a report linked to a table
- Create a report linked to a query
- Format data in a report
- Create logical expressions to find values in a specified range

Assignment Six

Night Vision database

Learning objectives

- Create a list box in a form
- Format labels and text boxes in a form
- Use and/or in a query
- Create labels using a report wizard

Assignment Seven

Tech Support database

Learning objectives

- Practise skills learned in Assignment Five and Assignment Six

Assignment Five

National Railways database

Scenario

Luke Thomas is the manager of the customer information service in a large railway station. He would like to provide customers with up-to-date information regarding the expected arrival time of trains.

In Assignment Five you will create a database to store data relating to trains arriving at the station. The queries and reports in the database will help Luke to find information on specific routes.

National Railways database

By completing this assignment, you will learn how to

- create a combo box to enter data in a form
- change the tab order in a form
- create a report linked to a table
- create a report linked to a query
- format data in a report
- create logical expressions to find values in a specified range.

Date and time fields

If you want to store a date or a time in a field, the data type for that field must be set to date/time in table design. Date/Time fields require 8 bytes of storage per field entry. Having set the data type to date/time, you must then choose an appropriate format. The format affects how the date or time is displayed. For example, the date 25/08/03 could be displayed as 25-Aug-2003, 25/08/2003 or Monday, August 25, 2003. The time 08:07 could be displayed as 08:07:00 AM, 08:07 AM or 08:07.

Shown in Figure 5.1 on page 50 is the Departure Time field, one of the fields to be created in this assignment. The data type of the Departure Time field has been set to Date/Time. Selecting a short time format means that only hours and minutes will be displayed.

Figure 5.1

 Task 1 Create a new database named **National Railways**.

Task 2 Create a table with appropriate field names and data types using the sample data shown in Table 5.1:

Table 5.1

Code	Date	Departure Time	From	Due in at	No of Stops	First Class	Restau-rant Car	Tickets Sold	Notes
KD001	25/08/03	08:07	Kildare	08:59	2	No	No	282	On time

Set the Code field as the primary key. Select short date as the format for the Date field and short time as the format for the Departure Time and Due in at fields. **Save the table as Train Schedule**. Do not enter data in the table at this point.

Numeric field types in Access

In the Riverside Rugby Club database, we used the byte number type to store whole numbers in the range 1 to 255. The remaining number types that we will encounter in the assignments in *Step by Step Databases* are listed in Table 5.2:

Table 5.2

Number Type	Description	No. of Decimals	Storage Size
Byte	Stores numbers from 0 to 255 (no fractions)	None	1 byte
Integer	Stores numbers from –32,768 to +32,767 (no fractions)	None	2 bytes
Long integer	Stores numbers greater than 32,767 (no fractions)	None	4 bytes
Single	Stores numbers with fractions	7	4 bytes

This table could be summarised as follows: if a field stores a number with a decimal element, e.g. 3.54 then the data type of that field must be set to number, and a field size of Single must be selected. The data type of a field that stores whole Numbers (numbers which don't have a decimal element) is set firstly to Number and then to either Byte, Integer or Long Integer depending on the size of the number. For whole numbers that will never be higher than 255 (e.g. a person's age) select the Number data type and select a field size of Byte. For whole numbers that may be higher than 255 but which will never be higher than 32,767 (e.g. the number of seats in a cinema) select the Number data type and select a field size of Integer. For whole numbers that may be higher than 32,767 (e.g. mileage on a car) select the Number data type and select a field size of Long Integer.

From this it can be seen that a field size of **Byte** should be selected for the **no of Stops** field and that a field size of **Integer** should be selected for the **Tickets Sold** field.

Task 3   Using the form wizard, create a form that includes all fields from the Train Schedule table, with columnar as the form layout and standard as the form style. The form title is **Enter Journey Details**. Design the form as shown in Figure 5.2:

Enter Journey Details

Code	☐	Date	☐
Departure Time	☐	From	☐
Due in at	☐	No of stops	0
First Class ☐		Tickets Sold:	0
Restaurant Car ☐			
	Notes ☐		

Figure 5.2

Combo boxes

There are many reasons why it is safer and more efficient to use a form for data entry rather than entering data directly in the table. One reason is the ability to restrict what the user can enter in a field by creating a combo box. A combo box is a drop-down list, which can be used for data entry in a form. Rather than entering data in a field by typing, the user selects the data from the combo box list. This has a number of advantages: data entry is quicker, spelling errors are eliminated and the user can be restricted to entering items displayed in the combo box. Combo boxes should only be used where there is a definite limit to what can be entered in a particular field. For example, a combo box could be used to enter data in a field called day, because the data entered in this field will be one of seven days.

Creating a combo box

1. View the design of the Enter Journey Details form, as shown in Figure 5.3:

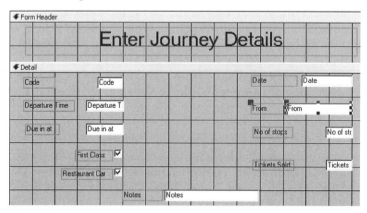

Figure 5.3

2. Click the From text box and press the delete button on the keyboard to delete the entire field.

Field List button

Figure 5.4

3. Click the field list button to display the fields in the Train Schedule table.

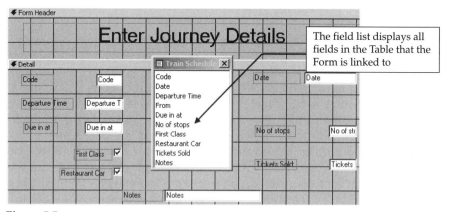

The field list displays all fields in the Table that the Form is linked to

Figure 5.5

Toolbox button

Figure 5.6

Figure 5.7

4. Click the toolbox button (if the toolbox isn't already displayed) and then click the combo box button. Drag the From field from the field list and drop it between Date and no of stops.

Figure 5.8

 Tip: Make sure the control wizard is on before you click the combo box button. If the wizard is turned off, Access will not bring you through the following steps. Control wizards can be turned on and off by clicking the control wizards button.

5. Select *I will type in the values that I want* and click next.
6. Type each location once in the list as shown in Figure 5.9:

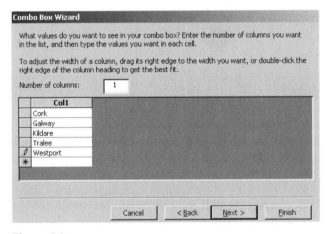

Figure 5.9

 (**Note:** Press the tab key or the down arrow key to move onto a new line. Pressing enter brings the wizard onto the next step.) When you have completed the list, click Next.

7. Ensure that 'Store that value in this field' is selected and that the field is From. Click Next.
8. Accept From as the label for the combo box by clicking Finish.

Figure 5.10

9. Click the properties button to view the properties of the combo box. Scroll through the properties until you find the Limit to List property. Set the Limit to List property to yes. This means that only items listed in the combo box can be entered in the From field.

10. Click the Form View button and then click the down arrow at the right-hand side of the From text box. You should get the following result:

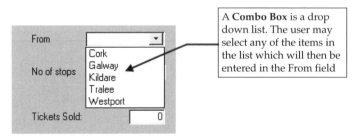

Figure 5.11

To enter data in the From field, select the text you require from the list shown in Figure 5.11. This has three advantages:

1. It is impossible to make a spelling error.
2. Data input is quicker because less typing is required.
3. The user is restricted to entering items displayed in the combo box list.

Changing the tab order in a form

The tab order determines the order in which the cursor moves from text box to text box in a form as you press the tab key. There should be a direct relationship between the order of fields as they appear on the form, the tab order of the form and how the data exists on paper before it is entered using the form. If all three are in sequence, the task of data entry is much easier. Often you will have to change the tab order to ensure that the cursor moves through the form in a particular sequence. When combo boxes are created in the form, the sequence of the tab order changes. Fields for which combo boxes were created are placed at the end of the tab order list, which puts them out of sequence. In the Enter Journey Details form, the cursor should move from Code to Date to Departure Time to From to Due in at, and so on. To see the current tab order of the form, firstly ensure that you are in design view and that the detail section of the form is selected. Now select **View** from the menu followed by **Tab Order**. The tab order should appear as shown in Figure 5.12 on page 55.

As you can see the **from** Field is out of sequence. **From** is the last field in the tab order but appears as the fourth field in the printed data. Once an item is selected in the from combo box, pressing the tab key will cause the cursor to jump to the next record. You would then have to go back to the previous record to enter data in the Due in at, No of Stops, First Class, Restaurant Car, Tickets Sold, Notes fields.

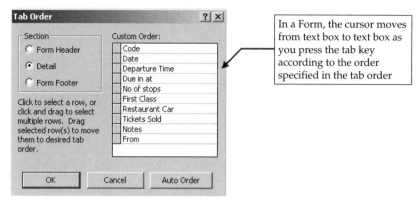

Figure 5.12

Rearrange the tab order list so that it matches the sequence of fields on the form and the sequence of data on the page as follows:

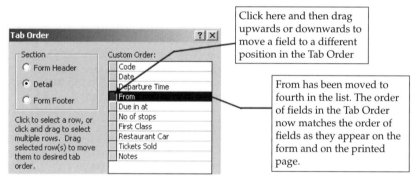

Figure 5.13

Figure 5.14

Task 4   Click the form view button and enter all the records shown in Table 5.3 on page 56.

Note: The records stored in the Train Schedule table will be in ascending order of Code, the primary key field, regardless of what order they are entered in the form. If you enter some of the records displayed in Table 5.3 in the form, close the form and then open it again later on, the records will not be displayed in the order in which they were entered. They will be in ascending alphabetical order of code. This makes it quite difficult to complete the data entry in separate sessions.

Table 5.3

Code	Date	Depar-ture Time	From	Due in at	No of Stops	First Class	Restau-rant Car	Tickets Sold	Notes
KD001	25/08/03	08:07	Kildare	08:59	2	No	No	282	On time
CD001	25/08/03	07:05	Cork	09:46	3	Yes	Yes	275	Running 10 mins late
KD002	25/08/03	09:24	Kildare	10:01	2	No	No	225	On time
GD001	25/08/03	07:45	Galway	10:26	4	Yes	Yes	298	On time
CD002	25/08/03	08:00	Cork	11:06	9	Yes	Yes	193	Running 20 mins late
CD003	25/08/03	09:05	Cork	12:27	7	No	No	270	On time
KD003	25/08/03	11:55	Kildare	12:44	2	No	No	187	On time
GD002	25/08/03	11:00	Galway	13:48	6	No	Yes	216	Delayed
TD001	25/08/03	09:15	Tralee	13:55	4	Yes	Yes	282	On time
KD004	25/08/03	13:06	Kildare	13:58	2	No	No	105	Cancelled
WD001	25/08/03	13:15	Westport	17:17	10	Yes	Yes	155	On time
CD004	25/08/03	14:25	Cork	17:26	9	Yes	Yes	180	On time
KD005	25/08/03	16:45	Kildare	17:37	2	No	No	196	Running 10 mins late
GD003	25/08/03	15:10	Galway	18:08	6	No	Yes	203	On time
TD002	25/08/03	13:48	Tralee	18:25	11	No	Yes	276	On time
KD006	25/08/03	18:30	Kildare	19:22	2	No	No	280	Delayed
CD005	25/08/03	17:30	Cork	20:16	3	Yes	No	270	Running 30 mins late
GD004	25/08/03	18:08	Galway	21:22	4	Yes	Yes	295	On time
WD002	25/08/03	18:00	Westport	22:01	10	No	No	301	On time
TD003	25/08/03	17:47	Tralee	22:41	11	No	Yes	320	Delayed

Figure 5.15

Figure 5.16

Task 5 With the Enter Journey Details form open, use the Find and Add New Record buttons to make the following changes:

1. The 09:05 train from Cork is running 5 minutes late. Enter this information in the Notes field.
2. The 15:10 train from Galway has been cancelled. Enter this information in the Notes field.
3. The departure time for the 13:48 from Tralee was incorrectly recorded. The correct departure time is 13:58 and the train is due to arrive at 18:35.
4. The 18:00 from Westport has a first class carriage and a restaurant car.
5. Another train from Kildare has been added to cope with demand. Enter the details shown in Table 5.4:

Table 5.4

Code	Date	Departure Time	From	Due in at	No of Stops	First Class	Restaurant Car	Tickets Sold	Notes
KD007	25/08/03	18:20	Kildare	19:12	2	No	No	225	On Time

Task 6 Create a query to find records of trains departing from Cork. Save the query as **trains from Cork**.

Task 7 Create a query to find records of trains departing from Kildare. Save the query as **trains from Kildare**.

Reports

People in business base their decisions on data they receive while they are at work. This data can come from lots of different sources such as business transactions, news reports and colleagues. Often this data has to be summarised and given a particular layout before it can be used as a basis for decision-making. By creating an Access report we can summarise, format and present data in a way that is easy to understand.

Rather than printing out data in the table or printing the results of a query, it is much better to use a report for a number of reasons:

1. The report can be formatted using font styles, sizes and colours.
2. A report title and introduction can be inserted at the top of the first page.
3. Functions can be used to perform calculations on the data contained in the report. For example, totals and averages can be calculated for numeric and currency fields.

4. Data contained in a report can be quickly sorted into different orders.

A report can be linked to either a table or a query. When a database has only one table, linking a report to the table means the report will display all records stored in the database. In the final section of *Step by Step Databases*, you will create a relational database, where reports can be linked to more than one table.

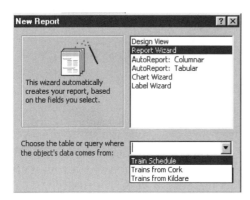

Creating a report linked to a table

In a single table database, all the records in the database can be displayed by creating a report that is linked to the table. In the following worked example, we will use the report wizard to create a report that displays data stored in the Train Schedule table. The report wizard helps you to create a report by asking you a series of questions. As you work through the report wizard, you will be asked what table or query contains the data to be displayed in the report, what fields should be included in the report, whether the report should be sorted and, if so, in what order. You will then be asked what formatting style should be applied to the report and how the report should be laid out on the page. Finally, you will be asked to enter a title for the report. In Access, the report title serves a dual purpose. It appears at the top of the first page of the report and it is also the name under which the report is saved.

1. Select Reports followed by New.

Figure 5.17

Access gives you the option of creating a report in design view or getting help from a wizard. Select Report Wizard, as shown in Figure 5.17.
2. Link the report to the Train Schedule table as shown in Figure 5.17 and then click OK.
3. The report wizard gives you the option of displaying some or all of the fields in the report. To add a field to a report, click the field in the available fields box and then click the single right-pointing arrow.

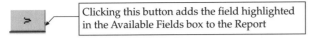

> Clicking this button adds the field highlighted
> in the Available Fields box to the Report

Figure 5.18

```
Report Wizard

                    Which fields do you want on your report?

                    You can choose from more than one table or query.

Tables/Queries

Table: Train Schedule        ▼

Available Fields:                    Selected Fields:

Code                          [≥]    From
Date                                 Departure Time
No of stops                  [>>]    Due in at
First Class                          Notes
Restaurant Car               [<]
Tickets Sold
                             [<<]

                    Cancel      < Back      Next >      Finish
```

Figure 5.19

4. Add the From, Departure Time, Due in at and Notes fields (in that order) as shown in Figure 5.19 and then click Next.
5. Click Next to skip grouping levels and Next again to skip sorting. (*Sorting will be introduced in Assignment Eight. Grouping will be introduced in Assignment Nine.*)
6. Click Next to accept tabular as the layout and portrait as the orientation.
7. Select Bold as the report style and click Next.
8. Type Details of All Trains as the report title and click Finish.

Fine-tuning report layout

Your report will look something like the extract from the completed report displayed in Figure 5.20:

```
Details of All Trains

From            Departure Time        Due in at Notes

Kildare            8:07                  8:59 On Time

Cork               7:05                  9:46 Running 10 mins late

Kildare            9:24                 10:01 On Time

Galway             7:45                 10:26 On Time
```

Figure 5.20

Each time you create a report, you will have to do some work to align the data below the headings and to position the data on the page.

As you can see, there is too much space between From and Departure Time, and the Departure and Due in at times need to be centred below the headings.

Design View button

Figure 5.21

Click the Design View button to display the report design.

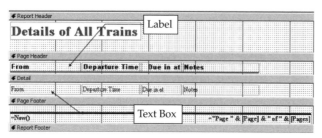

Figure 5.22

In the design report displayed in Figure 5.22, the label and text box of the From field are too wide. If this is the case in your report, select both the label and the text box by firstly clicking the label and then clicking the text box, while holding down the shift key. Position the mouse pointer over the middle dot on the right-hand edge of the From text box. When the pointer changes to a horizontal double arrow, click and drag to the left.

To centre Departure Time and Due in at, select the labels and text boxes for both these fields and then click the center button on the toolbar, shown in Figure 5.23 (*remember to hold down the shift key when selecting more than one label or text box*):

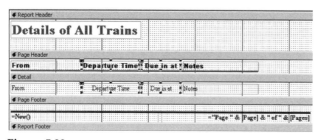

Figure 5.23

Print Preview button

Figure 5.24

Preview the report by clicking the Print Preview button. Departure Time and Due in at need to be moved to the left. With the labels and text boxes for both of these fields selected in report design, position the mouse pointer at the edge of a selected text box or label (but not above a dot). When the mouse pointer changes to the shape of a hand, drag the fields to the left to reposition them. The amended report design appears as follows:

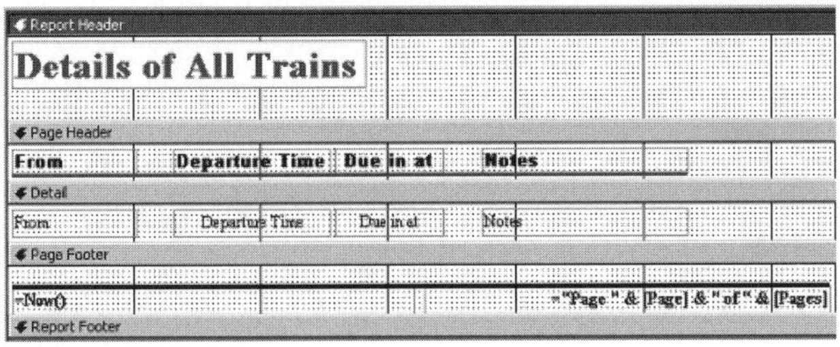

Figure 5.25

Preview the report. It should look something like the following:

Details of All Trains			
From	Departure Time	Due in at	Notes
Kildare	8:07	8:59	On Time
Cork	7:05	9:46	Running 10 mins late
Kildare	9:24	10:01	On Time
Galway	7:45	10:26	On Time

Figure 5.26

Creating a report linked to a query

If you only want to display specific records, as opposed to all the records, in a report, then the report must be linked to a query. The query must be created first in order to find the records that you want to display in the report. The report is then linked to the query using the report wizard. In the following worked example, we will create a Report that displays information relating to trains which have a first class carriage.

1. Create a new query to find records of trains with a first class carriage. Save the query as **Trains with first class carriage**.
2. Select Reports followed by New and then select Report Wizard. Link the report to the Trains with first class carriage query as shown in Figure 5.27 on page 62, and then click OK.
3. Add the Date, From, Departure Time, Due in at and No of Stops fields and then click Next.
4. Click Next to skip grouping and click Next again to skip sorting.
5. Choose tabular as the layout, portrait as the orientation and bold as the style.
6. The report title is List of First Class Trains.
7. Click Finish to preview the report.

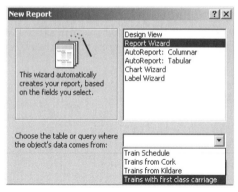

Figure 5.27

```
List of First Class Trains

Date From            Departure Time   Due in at   No. of Stops

23-01-02 Cork             7:05           9:46          3

23-01-02 Galway           7:45          10:26          4

23-01-02 Cork             8:00          11:06          9

23-01-02 Tralee           9:15          13:55          4
```

Figure 5.28

An extract from the report is shown in Figure 5.28. Click the Design View button and centre data in labels and text boxes for Date, Departure Time, Due in at and No of Stops. (Remember to select both the labels and text boxes by holding down shift on the keyboard.) Select the label and text box for the From field, and reduce the width (wait until the mouse shape changes to a double horizontal arrow). Now move both the label and the text box to the right (mouse shape of a hand) so that they are roughly half way between the date and departure time fields.

Figure 5.29 shows the report with the labels and text boxes for date, departure time, due in at and no of stops centred. The label and text box for the from field have been moved to the right.

```
List of First Class Trains

Date        From      Departure Time   Due in at   No. of Stops

23-01-02    Cork          7:05           9:46          3

23-01-02    Galway        7:45          10:26          4

23-01-02    Cork          8:00          11:06          9

23-01-02    Tralee        9:15          13:55          4
```

Figure 5.29

 Task 8   Display early trains from Cork using a report

- Create a query to find records of trains from Cork leaving before 12:00 am. Save the query as **Cork trains departing before 12:00 am**.

- Produce a report linked to this query. Include the Date, Departure Time and Due in at fields in the report.
- The report title is **Early trains from Cork**.
- Centre data in all labels and text boxes.

Task 9 Display express trains using a report

- Create a query to find records of train journeys with less than 4 stops. Save the query as **Journeys with less than 4 stops**.
- Produce a report linked to this query. Include all fields except for First Class and Restaurant Car in the report. Display the report in landscape orientation.
- The report title is **Express Trains**.
- Centre data in the labels in text boxes for Date, Departure Time, Due in at, No of Stops and Tickets Sold fields.
- Print this report.

Tip: If you are displaying a lot of fields in a report, add all the fields and then remove the fields you don't want to display in the report instead of adding each field individually. Fields can be removed from a report by clicking the single left pointing arrow in the report wizard.

Task 10 Display trains running to schedule using a report

- Create a query to find records of trains that are on time. Save the query as **Trains on time**.
- Create a report linked to this query. Include the Date, From and Due in at fields in the report.
- The report title is **Trains Running to Schedule**.
- Centre data in the Date and Due in at labels and text boxes. Resize and then move the From label and text box to the right.

Task 11 Display trains with a restaurant car using a report

- Create a query to find records of trains with a restaurant car. Save the query as **Restaurant car**.
- Create a report linked to this query. Include the Date, From, Departure Time, No of stops and First Class fields in the report.
- The report title is **Trains with a Restaurant Car**.
- Centre data in the labels in text boxes for Date, Departure Time, Due in at, No of Stops and First Class fields. Resize and then move the From label and text box to the right.
- Print this report.

Tip: If you want the report to display 'yes' or 'no' instead of a check box, open the Train Schedule table in design view and change the lookup of the First Class field from check box to text box before creating the report.

Using logical operators to find values in a specific range

In Assignment Three, we used the logical operator 'between' to find players who made between 5 and 8 tackles inclusive. **Between** is a useful logical operator if you want to include the lowest and highest number in the search results.

If you don't want to include the lowest and highest number in the search results, then you must use the greater than (>) logical operator and the less than (<) logical operator. The search can be made even more specific by using greater than or equal to (>=) and less than or equal to (<=).

Table 5.5

Logical Expression	Effect
Between 5 and 8	Finds 5, 6, 7 and 8
>5 and <8	Finds 6 and 7
>=5 and <8	Finds 5, 6 and 7
>5 and <=8	Finds 6, 7 and 8
>=5 and <=8	Finds 5, 6, 7 and 8

Notice that **between 5 and 8** and **>=5 and <=8** have the same effect.

Logical expressions can also be used for fields which store dates and for fields which store times.

Time fields

Table 5.6

Logical Expression	Effect
Between 10:00 and 12:00	Finds all times between 10:00 and 12:00 inclusive
>10:00 and <12:00	Finds all times from 10:01 to 11:59
>=10:00 and <12:00	Finds all times from 10:00 to 11:59
>10:00 and <=12:00	Finds all times from 10:01 to 12:00
>=10:00 and <=12:00	Finds all times between 10:00 and 12:00 inclusive

Date fields

Table 5.7

Logical expression	Effect
Between 23/01/2004 and 26/01/2004	Finds 23/01/2004, 24/01/2004, 25/01/2004 and 26/01/2004
>23/01/2004 and <26/01/2004	Finds 24/01/2004 and 25/01/2004
>=23/01/2004 and <26/01/2004	Finds 23/01/2004, 24/01/2004 and 25/01/2004
>23/01/2004 and <=26/01/2004	Finds 24/01/2004, 25/01/2004 and 26/01/2004
>=23/01/2004 and <=26/01/2004	Finds 23/01/2004, 24/01/2004, 25/01/2004 and 26/01/2004

Note: Access adds # to a logical expression entered in the query design grid that includes dates or times.

When you type >10:00 and <12:00 and press enter, the logical expression is displayed as >#10:00# and <#12:00#.

When you type >23/01/2002 and <26/01/2002 and press enter, the logical expression is displayed as >#23/01/2002# and <#26/01/2002#.

Dates and times are enclosed in # symbols. If you don't type the # symbols, Access puts them in for you.

Create a separate query for each of the tasks described in Table 5.8. Save each query using the name provided.

Table 5.8

	Purpose of Query	Query Name
Task 12	Find records of trains departing from 18:00 onwards	Trains departing from 18:00 onwards
Task 13	Find records of trains departing from Cork between 08:00 and 17:30 inclusive	Trains leaving Cork between 08:00 and 17:30 inclusive
Task 14	Find records of trains departing after 11:00 and before 18:00	Trains departing after 11:00 and before 18:00
Task 15	Find records of trains that are not on time	Trains that are not on time
Task 16	Find records of trains that haven't been cancelled	Trains that haven't been cancelled
Task 17	Find records of trains where the number of tickets sold was greater than or equal to 180 and less than 270	Trains with up to 10% profit
Task 18	Find records of trains from Kildare where the number of tickets sold was less than 200	Kildare trains for promotional campaign
Task 19	Find records of trains from Cork where the number of tickets sold was less than 250	Cork trains for promotional campaign
Task 20	Find records of trains from Galway where the number of tickets sold was less than 250	Galway trains for promotional campaign

Task 21 Complete the database structure form (Table 5.9) with data types and field sizes for all fields in the Train Schedule table.

Table 5.9

Field Name	Data Type	Field Size
Code		
Date		
Departure Time		
From		
Due in at		
No of Stops		
First Class		
Restaurant Car		
Tickets Sold		
Notes		

Ensure that the field sizes of text fields specified in design view of the train schedule Table match those specified in the database structure form.

Toolbar buttons introduced in Assignment Five

Figure 5.30

The **Field List** button: click this button to display a list of fields included in a form or report.

Figure 5.31

The **Combo Box** button: in form design, click this button to create a combo box.

Figure 5.32

The **Control Wizards** button: click this button to turn on the control wizard. When the control wizard is on, Access helps you to create a combo box, and other controls, by asking you a series of questions.

Figure 5.33

The **Properties** button: click this button to view the properties of an object in form design or report design.

Assignment Six

Night Vision database

Scenario

Siobhán O Sullivan works in the local video rentals store. She is new to the job and when customers ask her questions such as 'what comedies do you have on DVD?' she has to go searching for the answer. As new videos and DVDs are purchased by the store, they are entered in a ledger. Finding all films in a particular category necessitates scanning through the ledger from beginning to end.

In Assignment Six you will create a database to record details of videos and DVDs. The database will include queries and reports that will help Siobhán answer her customers' questions.

Night Vision database

By completing this assignment, you will learn how to

- create a list box in a form
- format labels and text boxes in a form
- use and/or in a query
- create labels using a report wizard.

Task 1   Create a new database named **Night Vision**.

Task 2   Create a table with appropriate field names and data types using the sample data shown in Table 6.1:

Table 6.1

Code	Title	Date Released	Rating	Running Time	Genre	Starring	Director	Format	Price per Night
DVD001	Jurassic Park 3	14/01/02	12	93	Action/ Adventure	Sam Neill	Joe Johnston	DVD	€4.50

Set the Code field as the primary key. **Save the table as Films in Stock**. Do not enter data in the table at this point.

Task 3 Using the form wizard, create a form that includes all fields from the films in stock table, with columnar as the form layout and standard as the form style. The form title is **Videos and DVDs for Rental**.

Task 4 Create separate combo boxes for the rating and genre fields. The values to be displayed in each combo box are shown in Table 6.2.

Table 6.2

Rating (Combo Box)	Genre (Combo Box)
18	Action/Adventure
15	Children's
12	Comedy
PG	Drama
U	Thriller
	War

Set the limit to list property to yes for both combo boxes.

 Tip: If you forget to drag the field from the field list when you are creating a combo box, data selected in the combo box will not be entered in the table.

 ## Using a list box to enter data

A list box is similar to a combo box. List boxes are used in forms and they allow the database user to enter data by selecting an item from a list instead of typing. However, with a list box all the possible field entries are displayed on the form. With a combo box, the possible field entries are not displayed until the user clicks the drop-down arrow. List boxes are useful where the number of possible field entries is limited to four or less, as a general rule. Combo boxes are useful where there are a higher number of possible field entries or where there is a limited amount of space available on the form. It is good practice to use a combination of combo and list boxes on a form as this adds variety to data entry.

Creating a list box

Follow these steps to create a list box for the Format field.

1. In design view of the Videos and DVDs for Rental form, click the Format text box and press delete on the keyboard.

Field List button		List Box button

Figure 6.1   Figure 6.2

2. Click the field list button to display the fields in the Films in Stock table and then click the list box button, which is part of the toolbox. Now drag the Format field from the field list and drop it in the detail section of the form.
3. Select 'I will type in the values' and create the list as follows:

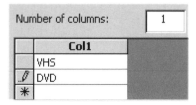

Figure 6.3

4. Click Next and ensure that the value is stored in the Format field.
5. Click Next and accept Format as the label for the list box.
6. Click Finish.

Add a label to the form header and rearrange labels and text boxes so that your form looks like the form displayed in Figure 6.4.

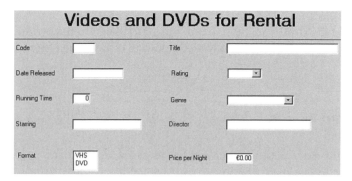

Figure 6.4

 Tip: Labels and text boxes can be aligned using the Format menu. Select the Code, Data Released, Running Time, Starring and Format text boxes. Select Format followed by Align from the menu and select Left. Repeat these steps for the Title, Rating, Genre, Director and Price per Night field.

 Editing labels in a form

Each field in the form consists of a label and a text box, as shown in Figure 6.5.

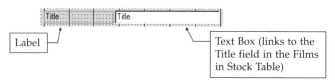

Figure 6.5

The label contains a description of the field while the text box contains the field name. The field name contained in the text box is the link between the form and the table and should never be changed. Changing the reference to a field name in a text box would break the link between the form and the table and, as a result, data would not be displayed in that field in the form. However, it is possible to edit the label because each label simply contains text. Editing labels to make them more descriptive makes the form more user friendly. In Figure 6.6, the label text has been changed from Title to Title of Film.

Figure 6.6

N.B. Never change the reference to a field name contained in a text box.

Changing the appearance of a form

When you create a form in Access, the default setting for the font is MS Sans Serif, font size 8. Changing the font size to 12 would make the data easier to read on the screen. Use of background colour and text colour can also make the form more attractive to the eye.

Formatting labels and text boxes

1. In design view of the Videos and DVDs for Rental form, select all the text boxes by holding down the shift key and clicking each text box once, as follows:

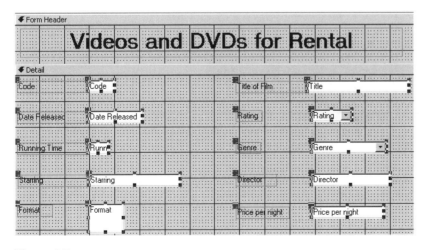

Figure 6.7

Formatting toolbar

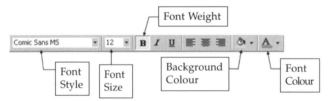

Figure 6.8

2. Select Comic Sans MS as the font style, 12 as the font size, bold as the font weight, a background colour of mustard and a font colour of navy from the formatting toolbar, displayed in Figure 6.8.
3. The height and the width of each text box must now be increased to accommodate the larger font size.

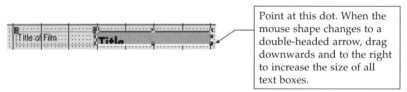

Point at this dot. When the mouse shape changes to a double-headed arrow, drag downwards and to the right to increase the size of all text boxes.

Figure 6.9

4. Select all the labels by clicking each label once while holding down the shift key. Format the labels as follows: font style=Book Antiqua, font size=12, font weight=bold, background colour=blue, font colour=white.
5. Change the border style of the labels by clicking the **special effect** button and selecting raised, as shown in Figure 6.10:

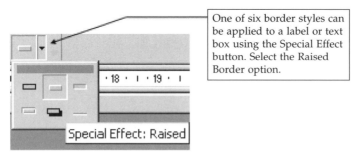

One of six border styles can be applied to a label or text box using the Special Effect button. Select the Raised Border option.

Special Effect: Raised

Figure 6.10

6. Increase the height and the width of each label to accommodate the larger font size.

Tip: You can make all your labels and text boxes the same height by specifying the height in the height property. In form design, select all the labels. Click the properties button. Specify the height in centimetres or inches (depending on how your computer is set up). Repeat this procedure for the text boxes.

Figure 6.11

7. Select the form header by clicking the text that says 'form header', shown in Figure 6.11, and then select green as the background colour.
8. Click in the detail section and set the tab order as follows: Code, Title, Date Released, Rating, Running Time, Genre, Starring, Director, Format, Price per Night. The completed form should look something like Figure 6.12 (notice how all labels and text boxes have been aligned and resized).

Videos and DVDs for Rental

Code		Title of Film	
Date Released		Rating	
Running Time	0	Genre	
Starring		Director	
Format	VHS DVD	Price per night	€0.00

Figure 6.12

 Task 5 Using the Videos and DVDs for Rental form, enter all the records shown in Table 6.3 on pages 74 and 75. When you have completed the data entry, continue with Task 6 below.

Task 6 With the Videos and DVDs for Rental form open use the Find Record, Delete Record and New Record buttons to make the following changes:

1. The rating for *The Mexican* is 15.
2. *The Mummy Returns* is on VHS and not DVD as recorded. The correct code for this film is VHS010.
3. The running time for *Evolution* is 102 minutes.
4. Due to a fall in rentals, *Freddy Got Fingered* is no longer being rented. Delete this record.
5. One new video and one new DVD have been added to stock. Assign an appropriate code to each and then click the new record button to enter both records shown in Table 6.4 on page 76.

Task 7 Create separate queries to find records of films rated U, PG, 12, 15 and 18. Save the queries as **Films rated U, Films rated PG, Films rated 12, Films rated 15** and **Films rated 18**. Print each query in landscape orientation.

Table 6.3

Code	Title	Date Released	Rating	Running Time	Genre	Starring	Director	Format	Price per Night
DVD001	Jurassic Park 3	14/01/02	12	93	Action/Adventure	Sam Neill	Joe Johnston	DVD	€ 4.50
DVD002	The Mexican	29/10/01	18	123	Comedy	Brad Pitt	Gore Verbinski	DVD	€ 4.50
DVD003	Captain Corelli's Mandolin	03/12/01	15	127	Drama	Nicolas Cage	John Madden	DVD	€ 4.00
DVD004	Shrek	12/11/01	U	112	Childrens	Mike Myers	Vicky Jenson	DVD	€ 4.50
DVD005	Miss Congeniality	12/11/01	12	106	Comedy	Sandra Bullock	Donald Petrie	DVD	€ 4.00
DVD006	The Mummy Returns	01/12/01	12	129	Action/Adventure	Brendan Fraser	Stephen Somers	DVD	€ 3.50
DVD007	Tigerland	26/11/01	18	97	War	Colin J. Farrell	Joel Schumacher	DVD	€ 4.50
DVD008	Evolution	26/11/01	12	122	Comedy	David Duchovny	Ivan Reitman	DVD	€ 4.00
DVD009	Along Came A Spider	05/11/01	15	98	Thriller	Morgan Freeman	Lee Tamahori	DVD	€ 4.50
DVD010	Blow	19/11/01	18	122	Drama	Johnny Depp	Ted Demme	DVD	€ 4.50
DVD011	Rush Hour	31/12/01	12	90	Action/Adventure	Jackie Chan	Brett Ratner	DVD	€ 3.50
VHS001	Cats and Dogs	03/12/01	PG	84	Childrens	Jeff Goldblum	Susan Perkins	VHS	€ 4.00

(Contd)

Table 6.3 *(Contd)*

Code	Title	Date Released	Rating	Running Time	Genre	Starring	Director	Format	Price per Night
VHS002	Tomb Raider	26/11/01	12	96	Action/Adventure	Angelina Jolie	Simon West	VHS	€4.00
VHS003	Freddy Got Fingered	14/01/01	18	83	Comedy	Tom Green	Tom Green	VHS	€4.00
VHS004	Down to Earth	24/12/01	12	84	Drama	Chris Rock	Chris Weltz	VHS	€3.50
VHS005	Briget Jones's Diary	01/12/01	15	93	Comedy	Hugh Grant	Sharon Maguire	VHS	€4.50
VHS006	Pearl Harbour	05/11/01	12	183	Drama	Ben Affleck	Michael Bay	VHS	€4.00
VHS007	Replicant	07/01/02	18	96	Action/Adventure	Jean-Claude Van Damme	Ringo Lam	VHS	€3.50
VHS008	Say It Isn't So	07/01/02	15	92	Comedy	Heather Graham	J.B. Rogers	VHS	€4.00
VHS009	Get Over It	07/01/02	12	87	Comedy	Kirsten Dunst	Tommy O'Haver	VHS	€4.00

Table 6.4

Code	Title	Date Released	Rating	Running Time	Genre	Starring	Director	Format	Price per Night
	Bloody Sunday	10/01/02	15	100	Drama	James Nesbitt	Paul Green-grass	VHS	€ 4.50
	Doctor Doolittle 2	26/01/02	PG	87	Comedy	Eddie Murphy	Steve Carr	DVD	€ 4.50

Creating queries with multiple conditions

So far, we have created queries with one or two conditions. In Task 7, we found films in different rating categories by entering U, PG, 12, 15 or 18 as a condition in the Rating field (*one condition*). In the National Railways database, we found all trains from Cork leaving before 12:00am (*two conditions*).

To find more specific information, more conditions can be added to a query, as shown in Table 6.5.

Table 6.5

1 Condition	Rating=12	Finds 9 records
2 Conditions	Rating=12 *Genre=Action/Adventure*	Finds 4 records
3 Conditions	Rating=12 *Genre=Action/Adventure* Format=DVD	Finds 2 records

The way in which conditions are 'joined' together in a query determines how many records the query will find. Conditions can be joined using the logical operator **AND**. Conditions can also be joined using the logical operator **OR**. Whether you join conditions with **AND** or **OR** greatly affects the results of the query.

Joining conditions using *AND*

When this method is used, the conditions are linked, e.g. films of DVD format which are comedies – **finds 4 records:** *The Mexican, Miss Congeniality, Evolution* and *Doctor Doolittle 2.*

Joining conditions using *OR*

When this method is used, the conditions are independent of each other, e.g. either films of DVD format or films which are comedies – **finds 16 records:** *The Mexican, Captain*

Corelli's Mandolin, Shrek, Briget Jones's Diary, Miss Congeniality, Tigerland, Evolution, Along Came A Spider, Blow, Say It Isn't So, Get Over It, Rush Hour, Doctor Doolittle 2, The Mummy Returns, Freddy Got Fingered and *Jurassic Park 3*.

From this example, it can be seen that whether you choose **AND** or **OR** to join conditions in a query determines how many records the query will find.

Table 6.6

Conditions	Conditions joined with	Number of records found
Format="DVD" Genre="Comedy"	AND	4
Format="DVD" Genre="Comedy"	OR	14

And logical operator

Conditions are linked (*the query shown in Figure 6.13 will only find films of DVD format if they are comedies*) **and are entered in different fields.** When creating the query *all conditions must be in the criteria line*. There is no need to type the word 'AND'. When Access sees more than one condition in the criteria line of the query design grid, it interprets these conditions as being joined using **AND**. The conditions displayed in Figure 6.13 would be interpreted as 'films of DVD format which are comedies'.

Field:	Genre	Format	Starring	Director
Table:	Videos and DVDs	Videos and DVDs	Videos and DVDs	Videos and DVDs
Sort:				
Show:	☑	☑	☑	☑
Criteria:	"Comedy"	"DVD"		
or:				

Figure 6.13

This query finds 4 records: *The Mexican, Miss Congeniality, Evolution* and *Doctor Doolittle 2*.

And conditions can be used on as many fields as you want. The more conditions you add to the query, the more refined the search becomes causing the query to find less records. The conditions displayed in Figure 6.14 would be interpreted as 'films of DVD format which are comedies and which are rated 12'.

Field:	Rating	Genre	Format	Starring	Director
Table:	Videos and DVDs	Videos and DVDs	Videos and DVDs	Videos and DVDs	Videos and DVDs
Sort:					
Show:	☑	☑	☑	☑	☑
Criteria:	"12"	"Comedy"	"DVD"		
or:					

Figure 6.14

This query finds 2 records: *Miss Congeniality* and *Evolution*.

Or condition (single field)

Conditions are independent of each other (*the query shown in Figure 6.15 will find films which are either drama or action/adventure*) **and are entered in the same field.** When creating the query *conditions are joined using or.* The conditions displayed in Figure 6.15 would be interpreted as 'films whose genre is either drama or action/ adventure'.

Field:	Genre	Format	Starring	Director
Table:	Videos and DVDs	Videos and DVDs	Videos and DVDs	Videos and DVDs
Sort:				
Show:	☑	☑	☑	☑
Criteria:	"Drama" Or "Action/Adventure"			
or:				

Figure 6.15

This query finds 10 records: *Jurassic Park 3, Tomb Raider, Captain Corelli's Mandolin, Down to Earth, The Mummy Returns, Pearl Harbour, Replicant, Blow, Rush Hour* and *Bloody Sunday.*

Or condition (multiple fields)

Conditions are independent of each other (*the query shown in Figure 6.16 will find films which are either PG or childrens*) **and are entered in different fields.** N.B. Conditions are not on the same line. The second condition is entered in the 'or:' line. With this type of query there is no need to type OR to join the conditions. The conditions displayed in Figure 6.16 would be interpreted as 'films whose rating is PG or whose genre is childrens'.

Field:	Rating	Genre	Format	Starring
Table:	Videos and DVDs	Videos and DVDs	Videos and DVDs	Videos and DVDs
Sort:				
Show:	☑	☑	☑	☑
Criteria:	"PG"			
or:		"Childrens"		

Figure 6.16

This query finds 3 records: *Cats and Dogs(Childrens rated PG), Shrek(Childrens rated U)* and *Doctor Doolittle 2(Comedy rated PG).*

Querying more than two fields using this method is not recommended. You may get unexpected or inaccurate results!

A mixture of *or* and *and*

Conditions are linked (*the query shown in Figure 6.17 will find films rated 12 which* *are either comedies or dramas)* **and are entered in different fields**. The conditions displayed in Figure 6.17 would be interpreted as 'films rated 12 which are either comedies or dramas'.

Field:	Rating	Genre	Format	Starring
Table:	Videos and DVDs	Videos and DVDs	Videos and DVDs	Videos and DVDs
Sort:				
Show:	☑	☑	☑	☑
Criteria:	"12"	"comedy" Or "drama"		
or:				

Figure 6.17

This query finds 5 records: *Down To Earth(Drama rated 12), Miss Congeniality(Comedy rated 12), Pearl Harbour(Drama rated 12), Evolution(Comedy rated 12)* and *Get Over It(Comedy rated 12)*.

 Tip: When entering text as a query condition, there is no need to type the inverted commas. Access does this for you.

 Task 8 Display DVDs rated 15 using a report.

• Create a query to find records of DVD films rated 15. Save the query as **DVDs rated 15**.
• Produce a report linked to this query. Include the Title, Genre, Starring and Price per Night fields in the report.
• The report title is **DVDs rated 15 Available for Rent**.
• Format the report as shown in Figure 6.18.

DVDs Rated 15 Available for Rent			
Title	Genre	Starring	Price per Night
The Mexican	Comedy	Brad Pitt	€4.50
Captain Corelli's Mandolin	Drama	Nicolas Cage	€4.00
Along Came A Spider	Thriller	Morgan Freeman	€4.50

Figure 6.18

 Task 9 Display videos for under €4 released in Dec 2001 using a report.

• Create a query to find records of VHS films released in December 2001 costing less than €4.00 per night. Save the query as **Videos for under €4 released Dec 01**.
• Produce a report linked to this query. Include the Title, Genre, Rating, Starring and Price per Night fields in the report.
• The report title is **Videos for under €4 Released in December 2001**.
• Format the report as shown in Figure 6.19 on page 80.

Videos for Under €4 Released in December 2001				
Title	Genre	Rating	Starring	Price per Night
Down To Earth	Drama	12	Chris Rock	€ 3.50
The Mummy Returns	Action/Adventure	12	Brendan Fraser	€ 3.50

Figure 6.19

 Tip: When creating a query with multiple conditions, add the first condition and then run the query to see if it works. Now add the second condition and run the query again. Add and test subsequent conditions one by one.

 Task 10 Display action/adventure and war films released Nov 01 using a report

    • Create a query to find records of action/adventure and war films released in November 2001. Save the query as **Action/adventure and war films released Nov 01**.
• Produce a report linked to this query. Include the Title, Genre, Format, Rating and Price per Night fields in the report.
• The report title is **Action/Adventure and War Films Released Nov 2001**.
• Format the report as shown in Figure 6.20.

Action/Adventure and War Films Released Nov 2001				
Title	Genre	Format	Rating	Price per Night
Tomb Raider	Action/Adventure	VHS	12	€ 4.00
Tigerland	War	DVD	18	€ 4.50

Figure 6.20

 Task 11 Display childrens/PG films available for rent using a report.

    •Create a query to find records of films which are rated PG or whose genre is childrens. Save the query as **Childrens/PG films**.
• Produce a report linked to this query. Include the Title, Rating, Running Time, Format and Price per Night fields in the report.
• The report title is **Childrens/PG Films Available For rent**.
• Format the report as shown in Figure 6.21 on page 81.

Childrens/PG Films Available for Rent				
Title	Rating	Running Time	Format	Price per Night
Cats and Dogs	PG	84	VHS	€ 4.00
Shrek	U	112	DVD	€ 4.50
Doctor Doolittle 2	PG	87	DVD	€ 4.50

Figure 6.21

Print this report in portrait orientation.

Creating labels with the label wizard

The label wizard is a report wizard specially designed to print data onto labels. This is particularly useful if you need to create product description labels, bar code labels, address labels or any other type of label. Once the labels have been printed, each label can be removed from the sheet and affixed to envelopes, ID badges, books, products etc. In the following worked example, we will use the label wizard to create product description labels for videos and DVDs.

1. In the database window select Reports followed by New and then select Label Wizard.
2. Link the label wizard to the Films in Stock table and then click OK.
3. The label type must now be selected from the list of available label types displayed by the Label Wizard. Each set of labels has a code number that tells Access the dimensions of individual labels and how many labels there are on each sheet of labels. For this exercise, we can print the labels on an A4 page so any code will do.

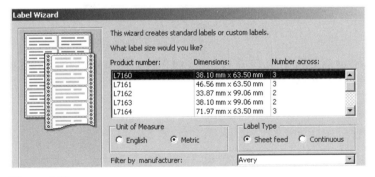

Figure 6.22

I have chosen L7160 because this code gives three labels across the page. (*If you want to print on actual labels rather than on a page, select the code that is printed on each page of labels. This code will also appear on the box the labels came in.*)

4. Click Next and select Times New Roman as the font name, 10 as the font size and a font weight of normal.
5. Click Next to go to the next step, which is where we define how text and fields are arranged on the label.

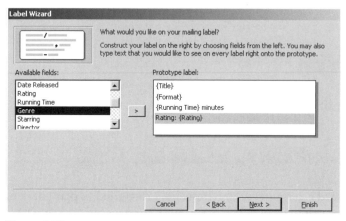

Figure 6.23

Set up the label as shown in Figure 6.23. Field names are in brackets and are added to the label by selecting the field in the Available fields box and then clicking the button with the greater than symbol. Press enter to move onto a new line before adding the next field. The text (minutes, rating:) is typed into the prototype label. Click Next when you have finished setting up the label.

6. Sort the labels by Format. Click Next.
7. Enter **Video and DVD labels** as the report name.
8. Click Finish to preview the labels.
9. Print the labels by clicking the print button or by selecting **File** followed by **Print**.

 Task 12 Using the label wizard, create labels for all films of VHS format.

 **Hint:** Create a query to find records of VHS films and then link the labels to the query.

Set up the label as shown in Figure 6.24. The report name is **Special Offer Labels**. Completed labels should look like Figure 6.25.

Prototype label:

{Format}
Special Offer: €2.00

Figure 6.24

```
VHS
Special Offer:€ 2.00
```

Figure 6.25

 Note: Database terminology is a little bit ambiguous here. A 'label' created with the label wizard should not be confused with a 'label' that displays descriptive text in a form or report.

 Task 13   Complete the database structure form in Table 6.7 with data types and field sizes for all fields in the Films in Stock table.

Table 6.7

Field Name	Data Type	Field Size
Code		
Title		
Date Released		
Rating		
Running Time		
Genre		
Starring		
Director		
Format		
Price per Night		

Ensure that the field sizes of text fields specified in design view of the Films in Stock table match those specified in the database structure form.

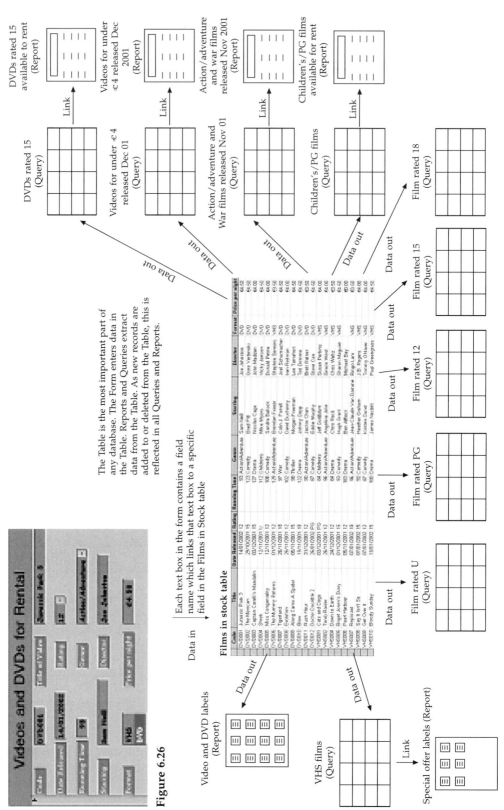

Figure 6.26

Figure 6.27

The Table is the most important part of any database. The Form enters data in the Table. Reports and Queries extract data from the Table. As new records are added to or deleted from the Table, this is reflected in all Queries and Reports.

Each text box in the form contains a field name which links that text box to a specific field in the Films in Stock table

How objects work together in a database

Figure 6.26 on page 84 displays all of the objects contained in the Night Vision database. Each object is in some way connected to the Films in Stock table. The Videos and DVDs for Rental form is used to enter data in the Films in Stock table. A number of queries and reports are used to extract data from the Films in Stock table. It is important to note that deleting a field in the table will cause an error in all objects that refer to that field.

Toolbar buttons introduced in Assignment Six

Figure 6.28

The **List Box** button: in form design click this button to create a list box.

Figure 6.29

The **Special Effect** button: in form design click this button to change the appearance of a label or text box.

Assignment Seven

Tech Support database

Scenario

Andrew Burke co-ordinates the technical support service in a software training college. In this type of college, PCs rapidly become obsolete and need to be upgraded regularly. Andrew is finding it very difficult to keep up-to-date lists of PCs by classroom. He also needs to be able to quickly determine which PCs currently need to be upgraded, but at the moment the only way of doing this is to go around the college, checking PCs and making a list of their specifications. In Assignment Seven you will create a database to store data relating to PCs currently in the college. A number of queries and reports will allow Andrew to get the information he needs with the click of a button.

Tech support database

By completing this assignment, you will

- practise skills learned in Assignment Five and Assignment Six.

Task 1 Create a new database named **Tech support.**

Task 2 Create a table with appropriate field names and data types using the sample data shown in Table 7.1:

Table 7.1

PC Number	Manuf	Model	Pro-cessor	Processor Speed Ghz	Hdisk Gb	Ram Mb	Sound Card	Speakers	Network Card	Date Pur-chased	Room No
1	Compaq	Presario	Pentium 4	1.8	40	128	Yes	Yes	Yes	20/05/03	12

Set the PC number field as the primary key. **Save the table as PCs.** Do not enter data in the table at this point.

Tip: For numeric fields with decimal places, it is best to set the decimal places to a fixed number in table design rather than leaving decimal places set to auto.

Task 3 Using the form wizard, create a form that includes all fields from the PCs table, with columnar as the form layout and standard as the form style. The form title is **College Computers**.

Task 4 Create separate combo boxes for the Processor, Processor Speed Ghz and Hdisk Gb fields. The values to be displayed in each combo box are shown in Table 7.2.

Table 7.2

Processor (Combo Box)	Processor Speed Ghz (Combo Box)	Hdisk Gb (Combo Box)
Pentium 2	2.0	40
Pentium 3	1.8	30
Pentium 4	1.7	20
	1.5	15
	1.4	10
	1.2	8
	1.0	6

Set the limit to list property of all combo boxes to yes. Change the label of the Hdisk Gb combo box to Hard Disk Gb.

Check the properties of the processor speed Ghz combo box in form design. Ensure that the format is fixed and decimal places is set to 1.

Task 5 Create separate list boxes for the Manuf, Ram Mb and Room No fields. The values to be displayed in each list box are shown in Table 7.3.

Table 7.3

Manuf (List Box)	Ram Mb (List Box)	Room No (List Box)
Compaq	128	12
Dell	64	12a
Sony	32	

Change the label of the manuf list box to manufacturer.

Task 6   Format all **labels** as follows:

Table 7.4

Height (except for Processor Speed Ghz which is 1.2 cm)	0.6 cm(0.24 inches)
Background Colour	Light Grey
Font Style	Times New Roman
Font Colour	Navy
Font Size	12
Font Weight	Bold
Special Effect	Shadowed

Task 7   Format all **text boxes** as follows:

Table 7.5

Height (except for list boxes)	0.6 cm(0.24 inches)
Background Colour	Dark Grey
Font Style	Arial
Font Colour	White
Font Size	12
Font Weight	Bold
Special Effect	Etched

Adjust the height of each list box so that all items in the list box are displayed without scroll bars.

Format Painter button

Figure 7.1

Tip: In form design, formats can be copied from one label to another or from one text box to another using the format painter. Select the label or text box that has already been formatted. Click the format painter button. The selected format will be applied to the next label or text box that you select.

Task 8 Draw a label box in the form header and enter the text COLLEGE COMPUTERS. Set the font size of the label box to 24.

The completed form should look something like the following:

COLLEGE COMPUTERS

PC Number	0		Manufacturer	Compaq Dell Sony
Model			Processor	
Processor Speed Ghz	0.0		Hard Disk Gb	0
Ram Mb	128 64 32		Sound Card Speakers Network Card	
Date Purchased			Room Number	12 12a

Figure 7.2

Task 9 Set up the tab order of the form in the following order: PC Number, Manuf, Model, Processor, Processor Speed Ghz, Hdisk Gb, Ram Mb, Sound Card, Speakers, Network Card, Date Purchased, Room No.

Task 10 Using the College Computers form, enter all the records shown in Table 7.6 on page 90. When you have completed the data entry, continue with Task 11 below.

Task 11 Create separate queries to find records of Compaq PCs, Dell PCs and Sony PCs. Save the queries as **Compaq PCs**, **Dell PCs** and **Sony PCs**. Print the records found by each query in landscape orientation.

Tip: Rather than creating each new query from scratch, view the design of an existing query, delete existing conditions, enter new conditions as required and then select **File** followed by **Save As** and enter the name for the new query.

Create a separate query for each of the tasks described in Table 7.7 on page 91. Save each query using the name provided.

Table 7.6

PC Number	Manuf	Model	Processor	Processor Speed Ghz	Hdisk Gb	Ram Mb	Sound Card	Speakers	Network Card	Date Purchased	Room No
1	Compaq	Presario	Pentium 4	1.8	40	128	Yes	Yes	Yes	20/05/03	12
2	Sony	Vaio	Pentium 3	1.2	10	64	Yes	No	No	14/09/01	12
3	Dell	Optiplex	Pentium 2	1.0	6	32	Yes	Yes	Yes	24/01/01	12
4	Dell	Inspiron	Pentium 3	1.5	10	64	Yes	Yes	Yes	14/09/01	12
5	Sony	Vaio	Pentium 4	1.7	20	128	No	No	No	21/10/02	12
6	Sony	Vaio	Pentium 4	1.7	30	128	Yes	No	No	15/01/03	12
7	Dell	Optiplex	Pentium 2	1.0	6	32	Yes	No	No	24/01/01	12
8	Dell	Dimension	Pentium 4	2.0	40	128	Yes	No	No	20/05/03	12
9	Dell	Optiplex	Pentium 2	1.0	8	64	Yes	Yes	No	24/01/01	12
10	Compaq	Presario	Pentium 3	1.4	10	64	Yes	Yes	No	18/02/02	12
11	Sony	Vaio	Pentium 4	1.7	20	128	No	No	No	21/10/02	12
12	Compaq	Presario	Pentium 4	1.8	40	128	Yes	Yes	No	20/05/03	12
13	Dell	Inspiron	Pentium 3	1.5	15	64	Yes	No	Yes	21/10/02	12a
14	Dell	Dimension	Pentium 4	2.0	40	128	Yes	Yes	Yes	20/05/03	12a
15	Sony	Vaio	Pentium 4	1.7	30	128	Yes	Yes	Yes	20/05/03	12a
16	Dell	Optiplex	Pentium 2	1.0	6	64	Yes	No	Yes	24/01/01	12a
17	Compaq	Presario	Pentium 3	1.4	10	64	Yes	No	Yes	18/02/02	12a
18	Dell	Inspiron	Pentium 3	1.5	15	64	Yes	Yes	Yes	21/10/02	12a
19	Dell	Optiplex	Pentium 2	1.0	6	64	Yes	Yes	Yes	24/01/01	12a
20	Compaq	Presario	Pentium 4	1.8	40	128	Yes	Yes	Yes	20/05/03	12a

Table 7.7

	Purpose of Query	*Query Name*
Task 12	Find records of PCs in room 12	PCs in room 12
Task 13	Find records of PCs in room 12a	PCs in room 12a
Task 14	Find records of both Pentium 2 and Pentium 3 PCs	Pentium 2 and Pentium 3 PCs
Task 15	Find records of PCs with both sound card and speakers	PCs with sound card and speakers
Task 16	Find records of Pentium 2 PCs with network cards	Pentium 2 PCs with network cards
Task 17	Find records of PCs purchased in 2001	PCs purchased in 2001
Task 18	Find records of PCs purchased in 2002	PCs purchased in 2002
Task 19	Find records of PCs purchased in 2003	PCs purchased in 2003
Task 20	Find records of PCs with more than 32Mb of Ram where the processor speed is greater than or equal to 1.0 Ghz and less than 1.5 Ghz	PCs for processor upgrades
Task 21	Find records of PCs purchased in either 2001 or 2002 currently in room 12a that have Pentium 2 processors	PCs moving to room 12
Task 22	Find records of both Pentium 2 and Pentium 3 PCs which either have no network card or have no speakers	PCs for speaker and network card upgrades

(**Hint:** In **Task 22**, both rows in the query design grid should have the same number of conditions.)

Task 23 Create labels for all PCs. The labels should include the PC number, processor speed Ghz, processor and date purchased fields. The report name is **PC labels**. Set up the labels as shown in Figure 7.3.

```
PC 1
1.8 Ghz Pentium 4
Purchased 20/05/2003
```

Figure 7.3

Print the labels either on an A4 page or on a sheet of laser labels.

Task 24 Display PCs in room 12 using a report.

- Produce a report linked to the PCs in room 12 query.
- Include the PC Number, Manuf, Model, Processor and Processor Speed Ghz fields in the report.
- The report title is **PCs in Room 12**.
- Align data in labels and text boxes where appropriate. In the label for the Manuf field change Manuf to Manufacturer.
- Print this report in portrait orientation.

Task 25 Display a complete list of PCs using a report.

- Produce a report which shows all PCs.
- Include the Manuf, Model, Processor, Processor Speed Ghz and Room No fields in the report.
- The report title is **Complete List of PCs**.
- Align data in labels and text boxes where appropriate.
- Print this report in portrait orientation.

Task 26 Complete this database structure form (Table 7.8) with data types and field sizes for all fields in the PCs table.

Table 7.8

Field Name	*Data Type*	*Field Size*
PC Number		
Manuf		
Model		
Processor		
Processor Speed Ghz		
Hdisk Gb		
Ram Mb		
Sound Card		
Speakers		
Network Card		
Date Purchased		
Room No		

Ensure that the field sizes of text fields specified in design view of the PCs table match those specified in the database structure form.

Toolbar buttons introduced in Assignment Seven

Figure 7.4

The **Format Painter** button: in design view of a form or report, click this button to copy the format of one object to another.

Progress test 2

Complete the test by writing answers in the space provided or by circling the correct answer.

1. Which of the following buttons is used to view the field list?

   a.

   Figure 7.5

   b.

   Figure 7.6

   c.

   Figure 7.7

   d.

   Figure 7.8

2. Complete Table 7.9 by entering the storage size in bytes required for each type of number.

Table 7.9

Number Type	Storage Size (bytes)
Byte	
Integer	
Long Integer	
Single	

3. List two advantages of using a combo box to enter data in a text field.

    a. _____

    b. _____

4. In Table 7.10, describe where each report section appears in a printed report. For example, the report header appears at the top of page 1.

Table 7.10

Report Section	Appears
Report Header	
Page Header	
Detail	
Page Footer	
Report Footer	

5. The logical expression **between 12 and 15** finds which of the following sets of numbers?

    a. 13, 14
    b. 12, 13, 14, 15
    c. 12, 13, 14
    d. 13, 14, 15

6. Write down the meaning of each logical operator in Table 7.11.

Table 7.11

Logical Operator	Meaning
<	
<=	
=	
>	
>=	
<>	

7. Each field displayed on a form normally consists of a text box and a label. Which one provides the connection between the form and the table?

    a. Text box
    b. Label

8. The table displayed stores details of cars.

Table 7.12

Registration	Colour	Model
00CE2079	Blue	Standard
03DL1830	Red	Sports
03KY2201	Yellow	Sports
02TN516	Red	Standard
03WX9031	Blue	Sports
02C6951	Yellow	Standard

How many records will be found by each of the following conditions?

Table 7.13

Condition	Number of Records
Colour=Blue	
Colour=Blue and Model=Standard	
Model=Sports and Colour=Red	
Colour=Red or Colour=Yellow	
Colour=Red or Yellow and Model=Standard	
Colour=Red or Blue and Model=Sports	

9. The field size of a date/time field is

    a. 1 byte
    b. 2 bytes
    c. 4 bytes
    d. 8 bytes

10. Which of the following buttons is used to create a list box?

    a.

Figure 7.9

b.

Figure 7.10

c.

Figure 7.11

d.

Figure 7.12

SECTION 3
Advanced Database Assignments

Assignment Eight

Southside Motor Tests database

Learning objective

- Use the autonumber data type
- Sort a report
- Create a parameter query
- Merge a database with a Word document
- Perform calculations in a report
- Use a wildcard in a query
- Use the **not** logical operator in a query

Assignment Nine

North West Challenge database

Learning objectives

- Use validation rules in a table
- Create a form linked to a query
- Create a grouped report
- Combine labels and text boxes in a report title

Assignment Ten

Southern Estate Agents database

Learning objectives

- Use the tab control in a form
- Create functions in a form
- Create a crosstab query
- Create a crosstab report

Assignment Eight

Southside Motor Tests database

Scenario

Southside Motor Tests provide a vehicle testing service for motorists in the south side of Dublin. Due to the high volume of tests the staff are unable to keep up with the huge amount of administration work.

In Assignment Eight you will create a database to store data relating to clients and their vehicles. Using the database you will streamline correspondence with clients with Mail Merge as well as producing a range of queries and reports to support the staff of Southside Motor Tests.

Southside Motor Tests database

By completing this assignment, you will learn how to

- use the autonumber data type
- sort a report
- create a parameter query
- merge a database with a Word document
- perform calculations in a report
- use a wildcard in a query
- use the **not** logical operator in a query.

The Autonumber data type

We have already used the number data type and set the field size of numbers to byte, integer, long integer or single depending on the highest value stored in a field and whether decimal places are required. With the number data type, the database user enters data in each field whose data type is number. An autonumber, on the other hand, is a number that Access generates for you. Once a field's data type is set to autonumber, no data entry is required in that field. For example, if a field named Order No was set to autonumber, Access would enter 1 as the Order No for the first record in the table, 2 as the Order No for the second record in the table, 3 as the Order No for the third record in the table and so on.

Autonumbers are particularly useful where there is a high volume of transactions and details of these transactions are stored in the database, with each transaction being identified by a unique number, such as an order number. In this type of scenario it is easy to make a mistake when entering an order number in the database. Time can also be wasted while looking for the last order number that was entered. Using an autonumber in this situation ensures that all records will be in sequence of order number without any gaps between order numbers. The need to keep track of order numbers already entered in the database is eliminated as this responsibility is taken over by Access.

The autonumber data type requires 8 bytes of storage.

Default values

A default value is where a value specified by the database designer is entered automatically in a particular field each time a new record is created. Default values are useful where the same value occurs frequently in a particular field. For example, in this assignment, Co. Dublin will be entered in every address3 field. To reduce the amount of data entry, Co. Dublin can be entered as the default value for the address3 field in table design.

 Task 1   Create a new database named **Southside Motor Tests**.

Task 2   Create a table with appropriate field names and data types using the sample data shown in Table 8.1 and Table 8.2. Use the autonumber data type for Test Number and set this field as the primary key.

Table 8.1

Test Number	Date of Test	Time of Test	Test Type	Reg No	Engine Size	Year of Manuf	Client First-Name	Client Surname	Address1
1	03/06/03	9:00	Full	95D30982	1.1	1995	Paul	Jenkins	25 The Avenue

Table 8.2

Address2	Address3	Cost	Test Result	Notes	Paid
Deansgrange	Co. Dublin	€48.00	Fail	Rear left brake light faulty	Yes

Enter Co. Dublin as the default value for the Address3 field. Save the table as **Test Details**. Do not enter data in the table at this point.

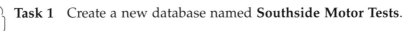 **Note:**   Access allows up to 255 characters to be entered in a text field. If you need to enter long descriptions in a field, such as patient notes in a medical database, the memo data type, which allows up to 64,000 characters, should be used. Because comments entered in the notes

field will not exceed 255 characters in this assignment, a data type of text can be used.

 Task 3 Set up a basic form linked to the Test Details table, using autoform: columnar. Save the form as **Client Booking Form**. View the properties of the form and change the caption property from Test Details to Client Bookings. (*The caption appears in the title bar of the window displaying a form.*)

Task 4 Create separate combo boxes for the Time of Test, Year of Manuf, Engine Size and Cost fields. The values to be displayed in each combo box are shown in Table 8.3.

Table 8.3

Time of Test (Combo Box)	Year of Manuf (Combo Box)	Engine Size (Combo Box)	Cost (Combo Box)
9:00	2000	1.0	48
9:30	1999	1.1	27
10:00	1998	1.2	
10:30	1997	1.3	
11:00	1996	1.4	
11:30	1995	1.5	
12:00	1994	1.6	
12:30	1993	1.8	
14:00	1992	2.0	
14:30	1991	2.2	
15:00	1990	2.5	
15:30	1989	2.8	
16:00		3.0	
16:30			
17:00			
17:30			
18:00			
18:30			

- Set the limit to list property of all combo boxes to yes. Check the properties of the Engine Size combo box in form design. Ensure that the format is fixed and decimal places is set to 1.
- Change the label of the Year of Manuf combo box to Year of Manufacture.
- Change the label of the Reg No field to Registration Number.

 Note: Because list boxes do not display currency formats, a combo box is required for the cost field.

 Task 5 Create list boxes for Test Type and Test Result. The values to be displayed in each list box are shown in Table 8.4.

Table 8.4

Test Type (List Box)	Test Result (List Box)
Full	Pass
Retest	Fail
	Fail Advisory

Task 6 Format all labels as follows:

Table 8.5

Height[1]	0.7 cm (0.28 inches)
Background Colour	Transparent
Font Style	Times New Roman
Font Colour	Navy
Font Size	12
Font Weight	Bold

[1]*Set the height of the Registration Number and Year of Manufacture labels to 1.4cm or 0.56 inches.*

Task 7 Format all text boxes as shown in Table 8.6.
Adjust the height of each list box so that all items in the list box are displayed without scroll bars.

Task 8 Draw a label box in the form header and enter the text Southside Motor Tests Ltd. Set the font size of the label box to 24 and the font weight to bold.

Table 8.6

Height (except for List Boxes)	0.7 cm (0.28 inches)
Background Colour	Dark Grey
Font Style	Arial
Font Colour	Mustard
Font Size	12
Font Weight	Bold
Special Effect	Sunken

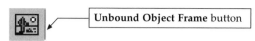 Unbound Object Frame button

Figure 8.1

Task 9 Display clip art in an unbound object frame.

In the Toolbox toolbar, click the unbound object frame button and draw a box in the form header to the right of the label. In the Insert Object dialog box, select Microsoft clip gallery from the object list. Click OK and then insert an image from the transportation category. View the properties of the unbound object frame and change the Size Mode property to Stretch. This resizes the picture so that it fits in the frame. Set the Back Style and Border Style properties to Transparent.

The completed form should look something like the following:

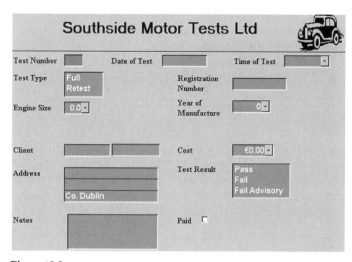

Figure 8.2

 Task 10 Set the Tab Order of the form as follows: Test Number, Date of Test, Time of Test, Test Type, Reg No, Engine Size, Year of Manuf, Client Firstname, Client Surname, Address1, Address2, Address3, Cost, Test Result, Notes, Paid.

Task 11   Edit the Client and Address labels as shown in Figure 8.2.

Task 12   Select the Test Number text box in form design. Click the properties button. Scroll through the list of properties until you find the Tab Stop property. Change the Tab Stop property from yes to no. This means that the cursor will not move to the Test Number field in the form as you press the tab key. The Test Number will be entered by Access as soon as the Date of Test is entered.

In previous assignments, we completed data entry in one step by entering data in every field for each record in the database. In practice, data entry will often occur in two or more steps because you may not have all the information needed to complete data entry until certain events occur. In Task 13 we will use the Client Booking form to register clients for tests by entering data in all fields except for Test Result, Notes and Paid. In reality, data relating to Test Results, Notes and Paid couldn't be entered at the time of registration because this data is generated by the test itself.

Task 13   Using the client booking form, enter all the records shown in Table 8.7 on page 105–06. Press the tab key to skip the Test Result, Notes and Paid fields. (**Note:** Data relating to Test Results, Notes and Paid will be entered at a later stage.) When you have completed the data entry, continue with Task 14 below.

Task 14   With the Client Booking form open, use the Find and Add New Record buttons to make the following changes:

1. Joe Reilly's test type is retest and the cost is €27.00.
2. Hugh Watson's car registration is 98D2096 and its year of manufacture is 1998.
3. Stephen Mc Carthy's test time has been changed to 15:00.
4. Martin Brennan's address is 15 Greenfort Close.
5. Two additional tests have been scheduled. Enter the details shown in Tables 8.8, 8.9, 8.10 and 8.11, on page 107 using the Client Booking form.

Sorting data using a report

One of the most powerful features of a database is the ability to display records in different orders. If the table has a primary key, the records will always be in ascending order of the primary key, but we may also want to view the records in a different order, e.g. ascending order of Date of Test or Client Surname. The easiest way to sort records is by using the report wizard.

Follow these steps to create a report in ascending order of Year of Manufacture:

1. Select reports followed by new. Now select report wizard, link the report to the Test Details table and click OK.
2. Add the Year of Manuf, Date of Test, Test Type, Reg No, Client Firstname and Client Surname fields. Click next.

Table 8.7

Test Number	Date of Test	Time of Test	Test Type	Reg No	Engine Size	Year of Manuf	Client First-name	Client Surname	Address1	Address2	Address3	Cost
1	03/06/2003	9:00	Full	95D30982	1.1	1995	Paul	Jenkins	25 The Avenue	Deansgrange	Co. Dublin	€ 48.00
2	03/06/2003	10:30	Full	97D201	1.3	1997	Keith	Morgan	54 Woodley Park	Blackrock	Co. Dublin	€ 48.00
3	03/06/2003	11:00	Full	98KE3398	1.6	1998	Andrew	Mooney	2 Prospect Drive	Blackrock	Co. Dublin	€ 48.00
4	03/06/2003	12:30	Retest	97D4071	1.0	1997	Jennifer	Butler	71 Seapark Court	Shankill	Co. Dublin	€ 27.00
5	03/06/2003	14:00	Retest	95D1556	1.3	1995	Maeve	O Shea	76 Forest Gardens	Killiney	Co. Dublin	€ 27.00
6	03/06/2003	15:00	Full	94WW692	1.8	1994	Liam	Dolan	68 Elmbrook Crescent	Dun Laoghaire	Co. Dublin	€ 48.00
7	03/06/2003	15:30	Retest	98D51223	1.1	1998	Thomas	Fennessey	12 Old Mill Road	Dun Laoghaire	Co. Dublin	€ 27.00
8	03/06/2003	16:30	Full	97D44981	1.4	1997	Joe	Reilly	84 The Moorings	Blackrock	Co. Dublin	€ 48.00
9	03/06/2003	17:00	Full	96LH8002	1.0	1996	Diarmuid	O Leary	2 Avondale Villas	Shankill	Co. Dublin	€ 48.00
10	04/06/2003	9:30	Full	95D10648	1.6	1995	Martin	Brennan	15 Greenfort Drive	Deansgrange	Co. Dublin	€ 48.00
11	04/06/2003	10:30	Retest	97D2096	1.6	1997	Hugh	Watson	10 Meadow Gardens	Blackrock	Co. Dublin	€ 27.00
12	04/06/2003	11:00	Full	98WW480	1.8	1998	Eoin	McCluskey	23 Parkvale Road	Blackrock	Co. Dublin	€ 48.00
13	04/06/2003	12:30	Full	98KE2948	2.0	1998	Stephen	Mc Carthy	34 Riverwood Court	Shankill	Co. Dublin	€ 48.00
14	04/06/2003	14:00	Full	90D639	1.3	1990	Rose	Corcoran	23 Beechhill Road	Deansgrange	Co. Dublin	€ 48.00

Table 8.7 *(Contd)*

Test Number	Date of Test	Time of Test	Test Type	Reg No	Engine Size	Year of Manuf	Client First-name	Client Surname	Address1	Address2	Address3	Cost
15	04/06/2003	14:30	Retest	94D36192	1.3	1994	Colette	Burke	27 Abbeywood Road	Killiney	Co. Dublin	€ 27.00
16	04/06/2003	15:30	Full	89D8087	1.6	1989	John	Cahill	12 Beechwood Road	Dun Laoghaire	Co. Dublin	€ 48.00
17	04/06/2003	16:00	Full	91WX1227	1.4	1991	Noleen	Higgins	20 Longwood Close	Shankill	Co. Dublin	€ 48.00
18	04/06/2003	16:30	Full	95D14933	1.1	1995	John	O Connell	1 Elm Tree Road	Blackrock	Co. Dublin	€ 48.00
19	04/06/2003	17:30	Retest	94KE6791	1.0	1994	Richard	Doherty	19 Larkhill Park	Dun Laoghaire	Co. Dublin	€ 27.00
20	04/06/2003	18:00	Full	90D2018	1.8	1990	Lisa	Burke	8 Clifden Road	Killiney	Co. Dublin	€ 48.00

Table 8.8

Test Number	Date of Test	Time of Test	Test Type	Reg No	Engine Size	Year of Manuf	Client First-name	Client Surname	Address1
2105/06/2003		9:00	Full	96D4487	1.0	1996	Ann	Moore	Deerpark	12 Heights

Table 8.9

Address2	Address3	Cost
Deansgrange	Co. Dublin	€ 48.00

Table 8.10

Test Number	Date of Test	Time of Test	Test Type	Reg No	Engine Size	Year of Manuf	Client First-Name	Client Surname	Address1
22	05/06/2003	9:30	Retest	97WW132	1.3	1997	Tim	O Neill	33 The Mews

Table 8.11

Address2	Address3	Cost
Shankill	Co. Dublin	€ 27.00

3. Skip the grouping step by clicking Next.
4. Select Year of Manuf as the field to sort by in ascending order and then click Next. *See Figure 8.3. (The report wizard default sort order is ascending (A–Z).*

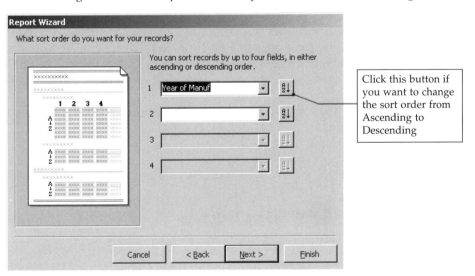

Figure 8.3

5. Select Tabular as the layout and Portrait as the orientation. Click Next.
6. Select Corporate as the style and then click Next.
7. Enter **Analysis of Vehicle Age** as the report title.
8. Click Finish to preview the report.

Analysis of Vehicle Age				
Year of Manufacture	Date of Test	Test Type	Registration Number	Client Name
1989	04/06/2003	Full	89D8087	John Cahill
1990	04/06/2003	Full	90D2018	Lisa Burke
1990	04/06/2003	Full	90D639	Rose Corcoran

Figure 8.4

Edit the labels in the page header so that they appear as shown in Figure 8.4, an extract from the report.

Note: When a particular year occurs a number of times in the Year of Manuf field, these records will appear together in the report. However, because a sort order wasn't specified for the client surname field, a group of records with the same year of manufacture will not be in any particular order of Client Surname. For this reason, Rose Corcoran may appear before Lisa Burke in your report.

Sorting by multiple fields

In the following example, we will create a report that is sorted firstly in ascending order of Date of Test (primary sort) and then in ascending order of Time of Test (secondary sort). This means that all tests occurring on the same date will be displayed in ascending order of time by the report.

1. Using the report wizard, produce a report, linked to the Test Details table that includes the Date of Test, Time of Test, Test Type, Reg No, Client Firstname and Client Surname fields. Skip grouping by clicking Next. Select Date of Test as the primary sort and Time of Test as the secondary sort, as shown in Figure 8.5 on page 109.
2. Select Tabular as the layout, Portrait as the orientation and Corporate as the style.
3. Enter **Test Schedule** as the report title.
4. Edit the labels in the page header and align labels and text boxes where necessary.

Creating a parameter query

If we wanted to find records of cars manufactured in 1998, we could create a query and enter 1998 as a condition in the Year of Manuf field. The problem

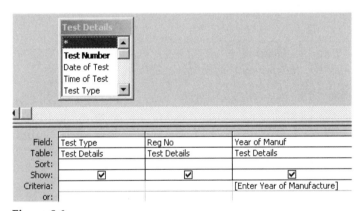

Figure 8.5

with this type of query is that we would then have to create separate queries to find records of cars manufactured in 1997, 1996, 1995 and so on. The solution is to create a query that prompts us to enter a year when the query is run and then finds records of cars manufactured in that year. This type of query, which prompts the user for input, is called a parameter query.

To create a parameter query, type a message, enclosed in square brackets, in the query design grid, as shown in Figure 8.6.

Field:	Test Type	Reg No	Year of Manuf
Table:	Test Details	Test Details	Test Details
Sort:			
Show:	☑	☑	☑
Criteria:			[Enter Year of Manufacture]
or:			

Figure 8.6

The text enclosed in square brackets will be displayed in an input box when the query is run, as shown in Figure 8.7.

Figure 8.7

The query will find records associated with the year of manufacture entered in the input box. A different year of manufacture can be entered each time the query is run.

Task 15 Create a parameter query which displays the message 'Enter client location' when it is run. The user can then type either Blackrock, Deansgrange, Dun Laoghaire, Killiney or Shankill. The query should find records matching the location entered by the user. Save the query as **Find clients by location**. Test the query by running it a number of times and entering each of the locations listed above.

 Tip: You must use square brackets in a parameter query.

Merging data with a Word document

One of the most useful features of a database is the ability to create a standard letter and link it to records stored in a table or query. This technique is used by direct mail marketing companies who promote their products and services through the postal system. In the following example we will create a standard letter, using Microsoft Word, and then merge the letter with the Test Details table to produce a separate letter for each client.

 1. Create the following document in Microsoft Word. (*Fields from the Southside Motor Tests database will be added later. The positions of the fields are indicated below. For the moment leave these sections blank.*)

Southside Motor Tests Ltd.
25 Gasket Road
Co. Dublin

> **Client Firstname Client Surname**
> **Address1**
> **Address2**
> **Address3**
> Fields will be inserted here

Our ref: | **Test No** field will be inserted here |

Dear | **Client Firstname** field will be inserted here |

The test for your vehicle, registration number | **Reg No** field will be inserted here | has been arranged for | **Date of Test** field will be inserted here | at

| **Time of Test** field will be inserted here |

Please arrive at the Test Centre at least 15 minutes before the test. If you are unable to attend the test at this time, please phone 209 6782 to rearrange your appointment.

The cost of the test is │ **Cost** field will be inserted here │ and can be paid by cash, cheque or credit card.

Yours faithfully,

John Murphy
Test Co-ordinator

2. Save the word processing document as **Test Notification**.
   Test notification.doc is referred to as the **Main document**. The table named Test Details is referred to as the **Data source** (*it contains the names, addresses and other details which will be added to the main document*). To produce a Mail Merge we must merge the main document with the data source. Because there are 22 client records stored in the Test Details table, the Mail Merge will produce 22 letters.
3. In Microsoft Word, ensure that the Test Notification file is open. Select **Tools** followed by **Mail Merge** from the menu. The following dialog box is displayed:

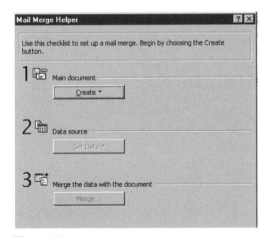

Figure 8.8

The Mail Merge helper, shown in Figure 8.8, identifies three steps required to implement a Mail Merge.

Step 1

Identify the document that will be merged with data stored in the database. This document is referred to as the main document. In this case the main document is Test Notification.doc.

Step 2

Identify the data that the main document is to be merged with. In this case the data is stored in a table named Test Details that is part of an Access database named Southside Motor Tests.mdb.

Step 3

Merge the main document with the data to create 22 letters – one letter for each record stored in the Test Details table.

4. **Identify the main document**
   Click the Create button, which appears in step 1 of the Mail Merge helper, select Form Letters and then Active Window. (*When you select Active Window, Word takes the document, which is currently open, to be the main document.*)

5. **Identify the data source**
   Click Get Data and then select open data source. Locate your database by changing Files of type to MS Access databases and by selecting the drive (hard drive, floppy drive, zip drive) and the directory where the database is stored. Once you have done this, the Southside Motor Tests data will appear in the Open Data Source dialog box.

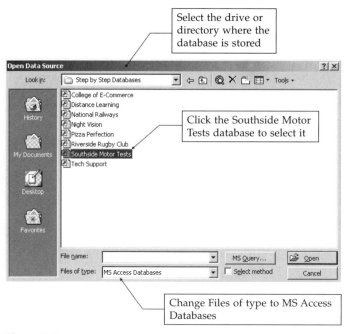

Figure 8.9

Select the Southside Motor Tests database and then click open.

6. Select the Test Details table and click OK. Then click Edit Main Document to insert the merge fields in Test Notification.doc.

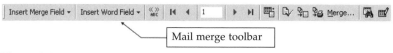

Figure 8.10

The Mail Merge toolbar appears below the standard and formatting toolbars. We now need to insert fields from the database in the Word document.

7. Position the cursor after the word Dublin and press enter twice to create a blank line and then click the align left button to move the cursor to the left of the page. Click the Insert Merge Field button and select Client Firstname. Press the spacebar and select the Client Surname field in the same way. Now press enter to move on to the next line and select the Address1 field using the Insert Merge Field button. Insert the remaining fields shown below in bold print in the same way.

Southside Motor Tests Ltd.
25 Gasket Road
Co. Dublin

<<Client Firstname>> <<Client Surname>>
<<Address1>>
<<Address2>>
<<Address3>>

Our ref: **<<Test Number>>**

Dear **<<Client Firstname>>**

The test for your vehicle, registration number **<<Reg No>>** has been arranged for **<<Date of Test>>** at **<<Time of Test>>**. Please arrive at the Test Centre at least 15 minutes before the test. If you are unable to attend the test at this time, please phone 209 6782 to rearrange your appointment. The cost of the test is **<<Cost>>** and can be paid by cash, cheque or credit card.

Yours faithfully,

_____

John Murphy
Test Co-ordinator

8. To complete the Mail Merge, select **Tools** followed by **Mail Merge** and then click the **Merge** button to merge all the records to a new document. The new document is called Form Letters1. It contains 22 pages. Each page is a letter to one of the 22 people selected from the Test Details table.
9. Save Form Letters1 as **March 2003 test notification letters**. Close all documents and exit Microsoft Word.

 Task 16   Using the label wizard in Access, create address labels (*as shown in Table 8.12 on page 114*) for the 22 letters. Each label should have the Client Firstname, Client Surname, Address1, Address2 and Address3 fields. Sort the labels in ascending order of client surname. Enter **Test Notification Labels** as the report name.

Table 8.12

Martin Brennan
15 Greenfort Close
Deansgrange
Co. Dublin

Set up the labels like this

Performing calculations in a report

In the following example we will create a report that displays the cost of each test and calculates the total cost of all 22 tests, using the sum function.

1. Create a report linked to the Test Details table including the Test Number, Client Firstname, Client Surname, Date of Test and Cost fields. Do not group or sort the report. Format the report using the corporate style. The report title is Analysis of Receipts Due. Click the design view button. The design of the report appears as shown in Figure 8.11.

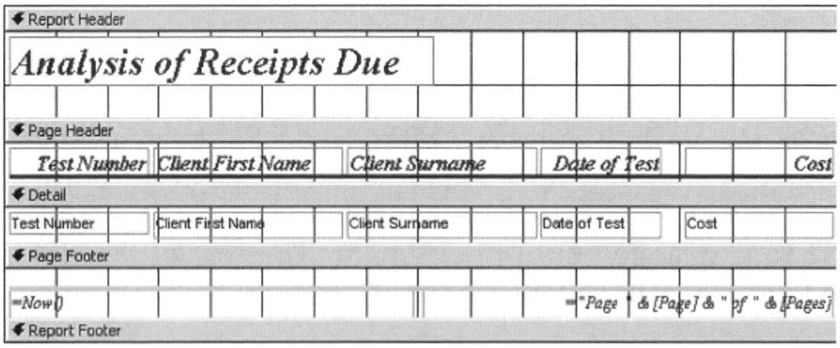

Figure 8.11

A standard Access report is divided into a number of sections.

The Report Header: This appears at the top of page 1 only. The report header usually contains the report title. It may also contain a brief introduction to the report.

The Page Header: This appears on the top of every page in the report except for page 1, where it is immediately below the report header. The page header normally contains the column headings.

The Detail Section: This is where the records contained in the report are displayed. The size of the detail section adjusts according to the number of records in the report. The detail section appears immediately below the page header.

The Page Footer: This appears at the bottom of every page in the report. The page footer normally contains the date and the page number.

The Report Footer: This appears on the last page of the report after the last record contained in the report. Functions, such as the sum function, can be added to the report footer. These functions perform calculations on data contained in the report. The report footer may also contain a summary paragraph or conclusion to the report.

 Note: In a one-page report, the report header and the report footer will both be on page 1.

The Analysis of Receipts Due report is displayed in Figure 8.12, with the positions of the report header, page header, detail section and page footer indicated. (*Data in labels has been edited and labels and text boxes have been aligned.*)

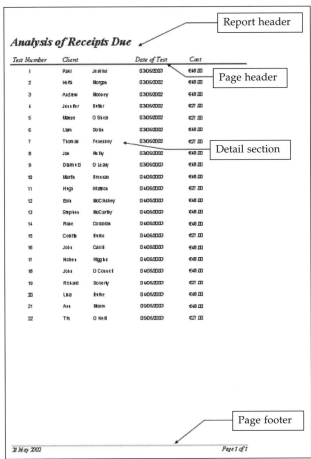

Figure 8.12

The report footer does not automatically appear in a report. In the next section, we will learn how to add a report footer to a report. We will also learn how to add report functions to the report footer.

Report functions

Report functions can be used to perform calculations based on data stored in a report. The functions are entered in text boxes in either the report footer or the report header.

Follow these steps to create a function that calculates the total of values stored in the cost field.

1. In design view of the Analysis of Receipts Due report, point at the bottom of the report footer bar and drag downwards until the report footer is about 1 inch high, shown as follows:

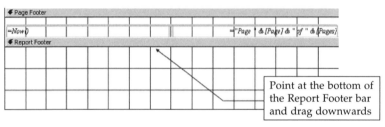

Figure 8.13

2. Click the toolbox button if the toolbox is not already displayed.

Figure 8.14

3. Click the text box button and drag downwards and to the right to draw a text box in the center of the report footer, shown in Figure 8.15.

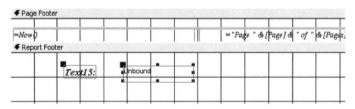

Figure 8.15

The text box appears just like a field. It has a label element, which in this case contains the text 'Text 15' and a text box element, which contains the text 'Unbound', meaning that it is not linked to any field in the table. Functions are always created in the unbound section of a text box.

1. Click on the word 'Unbound' and type the following function:

=sum([Cost])

2. Now click on 'Text 15' to select the label, highlight Text 15 and type Total Receipts Due in its place. (You may have to move the label to the left so that it does not obscure the function.)

Tip: To move a label independently of a text box, point at the dot at the top left of the label. When the mouse pointer changes to a pointing hand, click and drag to move the label.

3. Increase the font size of the label and the text box to 14 and adjust the height and width of both as necessary.

4. Click the print preview button to preview the report. The Total Receipts Due is 888.

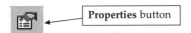

Properties button

Figure 8.16

5. In design view of the report, select the text box containing the sum function. Click the properties button to display the properties of the text box if they are not already displayed.

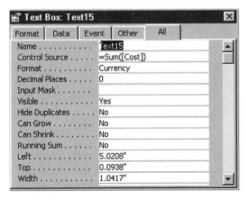

Figure 8.17

6. Change format to currency and decimal places to 0 as shown in Figure 8.17. Preview the report again. The Total Receipts Due now appear as €888.
7. Click the save button to save the report.

Note: Incorrect spelling of a field name referred to in a function causes errors. If a field name consists of more than one word, close attention should be paid to spelling and spacing when referring to that field in a function.

Structure of report functions

Each report function starts with = followed by the name of the function. Field names referred to by the function must be enclosed in square brackets [ ].

Table 8.13

Function Name	Action
=sum( )	Adds all values in a particular field that are displayed in a Report
=avg( )	Calculates the average of values in a particular field that are displayed in a report
=max( )	Finds the highest value in a particular field displayed in a Report
=min( )	Finds the lowest value in a particular field displayed in a Report
=count()	Counts the number of occurrences of values or text in a particular field displayed in a Report

Note: The sum and avg functions are normally used with fields whose data type is number or currency.

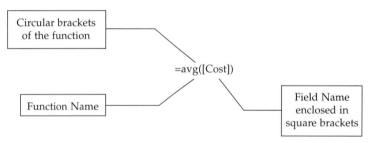

Figure 8.18

 Task 17   Calculate the average amount owed and total number of tests.

- Open the Analysis of Receipts Due report if it is not already open.
- Add the avg function to the report footer of the Analysis of Receipts Due report to calculate the average amount owed.
- Add the count function to calculate the number of tests carried out.
- Edit the properties of the text boxes so that the average is displayed in currency format with two decimal places and the number of tests is displayed as a number with no decimal places.
- Align the results of the calculations using the center button.

The report footer should look something like the following:

Figure 8.19

The average test cost is €40.36. There were 22 tests.

Tip: A quick method of creating a second function is to select the first function, click the copy button on the toolbar and immediately click paste. Edit the copy of the original function by changing the function name or field name as required and by changing the description contained in the label.

Task 18   Open the Client Booking form and enter data in the Test Results, Notes and Paid fields as shown in Table 8.14. (*The client firstnames and surnames have already been entered.*)

Table 8.14

Client First-name	Client Surname	Test Result	Notes	Paid
Paul	Jenkins	Fail	Rear left brake light faulty	Yes
Keith	Morgan	Fail Advisory	Replace side lamp bulb	No
Andrew	Mooney	Pass		Yes
Jennifer	Butler	Pass		Yes
Maeve	O Shea	Fail Advisory	Excessive exhaust emissions	No
Liam	Dolan	Pass		No
Thomas	Fennessey	Pass		Yes
Joe	Reilly	Pass		No
Diarmuid	O Leary	Fail	Front left full beam not working	Yes
Martin	Brennan	Pass		No
Hugh	Watson	Pass		No
Eoin	McCluskey	Fail Advisory	Re align headlights	Yes
Stephen	Mc Carthy	Pass		Yes
Rose	Corcoran	Pass		Yes
Colette	Burke	Pass		No
John	Cahill	Fail	Rear left indicator faulty	No
Noleen	Higgins	Pass		No
John	O Connell	Pass		Yes
Richard	Doherty	Pass		Yes
Lisa	Burke	Fail	Tyre tread not within specified limits	No
Ann	Moore	Fail Advisory	Oil leak	Yes
Tim	O Neill	Pass		No

Task 19   Create a query to find records of clients whose test result is fail. Save the query as **Failed Tests**.

Task 20   Create the following letter using Microsoft Word.

Southside Motor Tests Ltd.
25 Gasket Road
Co. Dublin

Our ref:
Dear

Your vehicle, registration number ———, did not pass its last test on and is now due for a retest. Please phone us on 209 6782 to arrange a time fo your retest

Yours faithfully

———————————————

John Murph
Test Co-ordinato

Save the letter as**Retest Notifications**. Using the Mail Merge facility set this lette up as a main document. Use the Failed Tests query as the data source and inser fields from the database, as shown in bold print below

Southside Motor Tests Ltd
25 Gasket Roa
Co. Dubli

<<Client_Firstname>> <<Client_Surname>
<<Address1>
<<Address2>
<<Address3>

Our ref: **<<Test_Number>**

Dear **<<Client_Firstname>>**

Your vehicle, registration number **<<Reg_No>>**, did not pass its last test o **<<Date_of_Test>>** and is now due for a retest. Please phone us on 209 6782 t arrange a time for your retest.

Yours faithfully,

————————————

John Murphy
Test Co-ordinator

Merge the main document with the data source to a new document. (*This document should have 4 retest notifications.*) Save this document as June 2003 retests.

Task 21   Display fail and fail advisory results using a report.

• In Microsoft Access, create a query to find records of results which were either fail or fail advisory. Save the query as **Test Result of Fail or Fail Advisory**.
• Produce a report linked to this query. Include the Client Firstname, Client Surname, Test Result, Date of Test, Reg No, Year of Manuf and Test Type fields in the report.
• Sort the report in ascending order of Test Result.
• The report title is **Clients whose Result is Fail or Fail Advisory**.
• Format the report as shown in the following extract:

Clients whose Result is Fail or Fail Advisory					
Client Name	Test Result	Date of Test	Registration Number	Year of Manufacture	Test Type
Lisa Burke	Fail	04/06/2003	90D2018	1990	Full
John Cahill	Fail	04/06/2003	89D8087	1989	Full
Diarmuid O Leary	Fail	03/06/2003	98LH8002	1996	Full

Figure 8.20

Use the count function in the report footer to calculate the total number of clients in this category. Format the label and text box as shown in Figure 8.21.

Number of clients in this category:	8

Figure 8.21

Tip: When you sort a report using the wizard, Access rearranges the order of fields in the report so that the sorted field or fields appear on the extreme left of the report. To prevent this from happening, do not sort the report using the wizard. Once the report has been created, view the design of the report, click the sorting and grouping button and then select the field to sort by and specify a sort order of either ascending or descending.

Sorting and Grouping button

Figure 8.22

Task 22   Display fail and fail advisory for 95–96 vehicles using a report.

• Create a query to find records of vehicles manufactured in 1995 or 1996 whose test result was either fail or fail advisory. Save the query as **Fail or Fail Advisory for 95 and 96 vehicles**.

- Produce a report linked to this query. Include the Client Firstname, Client Surname, Reg No, Date of Test, Year of Manuf and Test Result fields in the report.
- Sort the report in descending order of Year of Manuf.
- The report title is **Fail** or **fail advisory for 95 and 96 vehicles**.
- Format the report as in Task 21.
- Use the count function to calculate the number of vehicles in this category. Format the result as follows:

```
Number of vehicles in this category:    4
```

Figure 8.23

Task 23   Display overdue accounts from test passes using a report.

- Create a query to find records of clients who have passed the test but have not paid. Save the query as **Clients who passed but have not paid**.
- Produce a report linked to this query. Include the Client Firstname, Client Surname, Reg No, Date of Test and Cost fields in the report.
- Sort the report in ascending order of Client Surname.
- The report title is **Overdue Accounts from Test Passes**.
- Format the report as in Task 21.
- Use the sum function to calculate the total amount owed. Format the result as follows:

```
Total Amount Owed:    €252
```

Figure 8.24

Task 24   Display local clients with overdue accounts using a report.

- Create a query to find records of clients from Dun Laoghaire, Blackrock or Deansgrange who haven't paid. Save the query as **Local clients with overdue accounts**.
- Produce a report linked to this query. Include the Client Firstname, Client Surname, Address1, Address2 and Cost fields in the report.
- Sort the report in ascending order of Address2.
- The report title is **Collection List for Local Clients**.
- Use the count, sum and avg functions in the report footer to calculate the total number of fees to collect, the total amount to collect and the average amount owed, as shown in Figure 8.25.

```
Number of fees to collect:      6
  Total amount to collect:    € 246
  Average amount owed:        € 41
```

Figure 8.25

Task 25   Display records of vehicles matching the year of manufacture entered.

- Create a parameter query that displays the message 'Enter year of

manufacture' when it is run. The query should find records matching the year entered by the user. Save the query as **Vehicles by year of manufacture**.
* Create a report linked to this query. Include the Date of Test, Reg No, Engine Size, Test Result and Year of Manuf fields in the report.
* The report title is **Vehicles by Year of Manufacture**.
* View the report design.

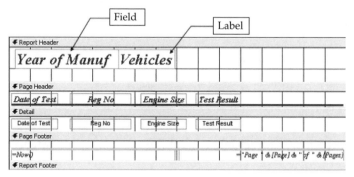

Figure 8.26

* In the report header change the label text from 'Vehicles by Year of Manufacture' to 'Vehicles'.
* Drag the Year of Manuf field from the detail section and position to the left of the label in the report header (*shown in Figure 8.26*).
* Delete the Year of Manuf label from the page header and format the report as shown in Figure 8.26.
* Resize the Year of Manuf field until it is just wide enough to display the year when the report is previewed.
* Sort the report in ascending order of Date of Test.
* Preview the report a number of times, entering a different year each time.

Task 26   Display records of vehicles matching the engine size entered.

* Create a parameter query that displays the message 'Enter engine size' when it is run. The query should find records matching the engine size entered by the user. Save the query as **Vehicles by engine size**.
* Create a report linked to this query. Include the Date of Test, Reg No, Test Result, Year of Manuf and Engine Size fields in the report.
* Sort the report in ascending order of Date of Test.
* In the report wizard enter **Test Results by Engine Size** as the report title.
* Change the report title to 'Litre Engine' in report design and add the Engine Size field to the report header, as shown in Figure 8.27 on page 124 where 1.1 was entered as the engine size when previewing the report.

Preview the report a number of times, entering a different engine size each time.

1.1 Litre Engine			
Date of Test	Reg. No.	Test Result	Year of Manufacture
03/06/2002	98D51223	Pass	1998
03/06/2003	95D30982	Fail	1995
04/06/2003	95D14933	Pass	1995

Figure 8.27

 Tip: The report title entered in the report wizard is also used by Access as the report name.

 Task 27   Display records of vehicles matching the test result entered.

- Create a parameter query which displays the message 'Enter test result' when it is run. The query should find records matching the test result entered by the user. Save the query as **Results by category**.
- Create a report linked to this query. Include the Test Result, Date of Test, Reg No, Engine Size and Year of Manuf fields in the report.
- Sort the report in ascending order of Date of Test.
- In the report wizard enter **Test Results by Category** as the report title.
- In report design, delete the report title and replace it with the Test Result field, as shown in Figure 8.28, where Fail Advisory was entered in the parameter value dialog box.

Fail Advisory			
Date of Test	Reg. No.	Engine Size	Year of Manufacture
03/06/2002	95D1556	1.3	1995
03/06/2002	97D201	1.3	1997
04/06/2003	98WW480	1.8	1998
05/06/2003	96D4487	1	1996

Figure 8.28

Preview the report a number of times, entering a different test result each time.

 ## Wildcards

A wildcard is very useful if you are looking for a particular record or records but do not have all the details of that record to hand. For example, if you are looking for details of a particular vehicle and you only know that the last number of the registration is 1, a wildcard query can be created to find details of all vehicles whose registration number ends with 1.

The * symbol is used in a wildcard query to indicate the part of the text or number that we are unsure of and is combined with a piece of information to create a search string. The position of the * in the search string is very important.
Table 8.15 *Example (relating to the Reg No field)*

Table 8.15

Search String	Meaning	Finds
*1	We know the registration ends in the number 1 but do not know what comes before the number	97D201, 97D4071, 97D44981 and 94KE6791
95*	We know the registration starts with 95 but do not know what comes after 95	95D30982, 95D1556, 95D10648 and 95D14933

Positioning the * at the beginning of the search string means 'find everything that ends with'. For example, *y means 'find all text that ends with y', *th means 'find all text that ends with th', *8 means 'find all numbers or text ending with 8'.

Positioning the * at the end of the search string means 'find everything that begins with'. For example, D* means 'find all text that begins with D', Sl* means 'find all text that begins with Sl', 6* means 'find all numbers or text that begin with 6'.

Using a wildcard in a query

In the following example, we will create a query to find records of vehicles whose registration begins with 95.

1. Create a new query and add all the fields to the query design grid.
2. In the criteria for Reg No, type **95*** and press enter.

Field:	Test Type	Reg No	Engine Size
Table:	Test Details	Test Details	Test Details
Sort:			
Show:	☑	☑	☑
Criteria:		Like "95*"	
or:			

Figure 8.29

Access edits the formula as shown in Figure 8.29. (*There is no need to type Like or to enclose the search string in inverted commas. Access does this for you when you press enter.*)

3. Run the query. It should find 4 records. Save the query as **Registrations beginning with 95.**

Using *Not* with a wildcard

The not logical operator can be combined with a wildcard in a query condition. If, for example, we wanted to find all cars except for those registered in 1995, we would have to create a query condition that finds all records where the car registration does not begin with 95.

In the following example, we will create a query to find records of vehicles except for those whose registration begins with 95.

1. Create a new query and add all the fields to the query design grid.
2. In the criteria for Reg No type **not 95*** and press enter.
   Access edits the formula as shown in Figure 8.30. (*As before, there is no need to type Like or to enclose the search string in inverted commas.*)

Field:	Test Type	Reg No	Engine Size
Table:	Test Details	Test Details	Test Details
Sort:			
Show:	✔	✔	✔
Criteria:		Not Like "95*"	
or:			

Figure 8.30

3. Run the query. It should find 18 records. Save the query as **All vehicles except for those registered in 1995**.

Create a separate query for each of the tasks described in Table 8.16. Save each query using the name provided.

Table 8.16

	Purpose of Query	*Query Name*
Task 28	Find records of vehicles whose registration begins with 94	Registrations beginning with 94
Task 29	Find records of vehicles whose registration ends with 8	Registrations ending in 8
Task 30	Find records of all clients whose address begins with the number 2	Address begins with 2
Task 31	Find records of clients whose address includes the word 'Road'	Address includes Road
Task 32	Find records of clients whose address does not end with the word 'Court'	Address does not end with Court
Task 33	Find records of clients whose surname does not begin with 'Mc'	Surname does not begin with Mc
Task 34	Find records of vehicles whose registration does not end with 1, 2 or 3	Registration does not end with 1, 2 or 3

Task 35 Complete the following database structure form with data types and field sizes for all fields in the Test Details table:

Table 8.17

Field Name	Data Type	Field Size
Test Number		
Date of Test		
Time of Test		
Test Type		
Reg No		
Engine Size		
Year of Manuf		
Client Firstname		
Client Surname		
Address1		
Address2		
Address3		
Cost		
Test Result		
Notes		
Paid		

Ensure that the field sizes of text fields specified in design view of the Test Details table match those specified in the database structure form.

Toolbar buttons introduced in Assignment Eight

Figure 8.31

The **Text Box** button: the text box button is used for creating functions and formulas. In report design, click this button and drag downwards and to the right to create a text box in the report footer. Text boxes can also be created in the report header.

Figure 8.32

The **Unbound Object Frame** button: in design view of a form or report, click this button and draw a box to insert a picture or clip art.

Figure 8.33

The **Sorting and Grouping** button: click this button in report design to sort the report in ascending or descending order by a selected field or fields.

Assignment Nine

North West Challenge database

Scenario

Mick Byrne and Joe Doyle are keen hill walkers. They have set themselves the challenge of climbing all the mountains that are higher than 600 metres in the north west. In Assignment Nine, you will create a database to keep track of their progress. The database will help Mick and Joe to plan each weekend of hill-walking as well as producing reports detailing mountains which they have already climbed.

North West Challenge database

By completing this assignment, you will learn how to

- use validation rules in a table
- create a form linked to a query
- create a grouped report
- combine labels and text boxes in a report title.

Task 1   Create a new database named **North West Challenge**.

Task 2   Create a table with appropriate field names and data types using the sample data shown in Table 9.1.

Table 9.1

Mountain Number	Name of Mountain	Height (Metres)	County	Province	Map Number	Date Climbed	Group Members
1	Croaghan	925	Mayo	Connaught	30	30/05/2003	Mick Byrne, Joe Doyle

Set the Mountain Number field as the primary key. Set the default value of the Province field to Connaught. Save the table as **600 Metre Mountains**. Do not enter data in the table at this point.

Data validation

Data validation allows you to restrict the type of data that is entered in a particular field and reduce the possibility of data entry errors. Data validation can be used for numeric fields where numbers will always occur within a certain range. For example, a person's age will always be between 0 and 110. For text fields, data validation can be used where there is a definite limit to what can be entered in a particular field. For example, only Munster, Leinster, Connaught or Ulster could be entered in a field named province.

Data validation is implemented by creating a logical expression, which is entered as a validation rule in table design. Validation text is also entered for each validation rule. The validation text is a message that will be displayed if the user attempts to enter data that breaks the validation rule.

Examples

Table 9.2

Validation Rule	Validation Text	Effect
Between 0 and 110	Please enter a number between 0 and 110	The message 'Please enter a number between 0 and 110' is displayed if the user tries to enter a number which is less than 0 or greater than 110
'Munster' or 'Leinster' or 'Connaught' or 'Ulster'	Please enter a valid province name	The message 'Please enter a valid province name' is displayed if the user tries to enter anything other than Munster, Leinster, Ulster or Connaught

In the following example, we will create a validation rule for the Height (Metres) field. All the mountains stored in the 600 Metre Mountains table are at least 600 metres high. The highest mountain in Ireland is 1039 metres high. Our validation rule will prevent the user from entering a number which is less than 600 or greater than 1039 in the Height (Metres) field using the logical expression 'Between 600 and 1039'.

1. In design view of the 600 Metre Mountains table, click the Height (Metres) field to select it, as shown in Figure 9.1 on page 131.
2. In validation rule type **Between 600 and 1039** as shown in Figure 9.1. This means that only numbers between 600 and 1039 inclusive will be accepted in this field.
3. In validation text type **Please enter a number in the range 600–1039**. This is an error message which will appear if the user tries to enter a number less than 600 or a number greater than 1039.

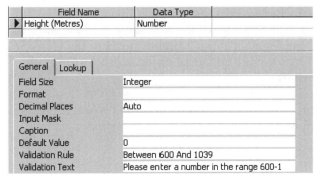

Figure 9.1

 Task 3 Create a validation rule for the Map Number field as follows:

Table 9.3

Field	Validation Rule	Validation Text
Map Number	Between 1 and 100	Please enter a number in the range 1–100

▦ Datasheet View

Figure 9.2

Save the changes to the design of the 600 Metre Mountains table. Click the datasheet view button and test both validation rules by entering data outside of the allowed range in the Height (Metres) and Map Number fields. (*For example, try entering 2500 in the Height (Metres) field and then try entering 125 in the Map Number field.*) The validation text should be displayed as an error message. Click OK and then press esc twice to cancel the data entry.

Data entry

In this assignment data entry will occur in two stages:

Stage 1: Data will be entered in the Mountain Number, Name of Mountain, Height (Metres), County, Province and Map Number fields for all mountains which Mick and Joe intend to climb.

Stage 2: As Mick and Joe climb the mountains data will be entered in the Date Climbed and Group Members fields.

In the Southside Motor Tests database data entry also required two stages. Both stages of the data entry were implemented using one form. In the North West Challenge database, we will use a separate form for each stage of data entry.

Task 4 Using the form wizard, create a form linked to the 600 Metre Mountains table. Add the Mountain Number, Name of Mountain, Height (Metres), County, Province and Map Number fields to the form. Select columnar as the form layout and expedition as the form style. The form title is **North West Mountains**.

Task 5 Create separate combo boxes for the County and Map Number fields. The values to be displayed in each combo box are shown in Table 9.4.

Table 9.4

County (Combo Box)	Map Number (Combo Box)
Derry	1
Donegal	2
Mayo	3
Sligo	6
	11
	13
	16
	23
	26
	30
	31

Set the limit to list property to yes for both combo boxes.

Task 6 Create a list box for Province. The values to be displayed in the list box are shown in Table 9.5.

Table 9.5

Province (List Box)
Connaught
Ulster

Task 7 Select all text boxes and set the font size to 12 and the font weight to bold. Set the height of all text boxes (*except for Province*) to 0.6 cm (0.24 inches).

Task 8   Select all labels and set the font size to 12. Edit the Height (Metres) label so that it reads 'Height in Metres'.

Task 9   Draw a label box in the form header and enter the text North West Mountains. Change the font style of this label to Book Antiqua and set the font size to 28. Insert clip art from the navigation category in the form header as shown in Figure 9.3.
   The completed form should look something like the following:

North West Mountains

Mountain Number	1	Name of Mountain	Croaghan
Height in Metres	925	County	Mayo
Province	Connaught / Ulster	Map Number	30

Figure 9.3

Note: The height of the Province, County and Map Number labels is 0.6 cm. The height of the Mountain Number, Name of Mountain and Height in Metres labels is 1.2 cm.

Task 10   Set up the tab order of the form as follows: Mountain Number, Name of Mountain, Height (Metres), County, Province, Map Mumber.

Task 11   Using the North West Mountains form, enter all the records shown in Table 9.6 on page 134. When you have completed the data entry, continue with Task 12 below.

Task 12   Create a parameter query which displays the message 'Enter name of county' when it is run. The query should then find records of 600 metre mountains in the county entered by the user. Save the query as **600 metre mountains by county**.

Task 13 Display records of mountains matching the county entered.

• Create a report linked to the 600 metre mountains by county query using the report wizard. Include the Name of Mountain, Height (Metres), Map Number and County fields in the report.
• Sort the report in descending order of Height (Metres).
• Select tabular as the layout, portrait as the orientation and casual as the report style.
• The report title is **Mountains by County**.

Table 9.6

Mountain Number	Name of Mountain	Height (Metres)	County	Province	Map Number
1	Croaghan	925	Mayo	Connaught	30
2	Croagh Patrick	764	Mayo	Connaught	30
3	Tonacroaghaun	688	Mayo	Connaught	30
4	Slievemore	671	Mayo	Connaught	30
5	Corranabinnia	716	Mayo	Connaught	30
6	Glennamong	628	Mayo	Connaught	30
7	Nephin Beg	627	Mayo	Connaught	23
8	Slieve Car	721	Mayo	Connaught	23
9	Birreencorragh	698	Mayo	Connaught	31
10	Nephin	806	Mayo	Connaught	31
11	Truskmore	647	Sligo	Connaught	16
12	Tievebaun	611	Sligo	Connaught	16
13	Cuilcagh	665	Sligo	Connaught	26
14	Muckish	666	Donegal	Ulster	2
15	Aghla Beg	603	Donegal	Ulster	2
16	Errigal	751	Donegal	Ulster	1
17	Slieve Snaght	678	Donegal	Ulster	1
18	Dooish	652	Donegal	Ulster	6
19	Silver Hill	600	Donegal	Ulster	11
20	Lavagh Beg	650	Donegal	Ulster	11
21	Lavagh More	671	Donegal	Ulster	11
22	Croaghgorm	674	Donegal	Ulster	11
23	Knockgorm	642	Donegal	Ulster	11
24	Ardnageer	626	Donegal	Ulster	11
25	Croaghbane	641	Donegal	Ulster	11
26	Mullaghclocha	635	Derry	Ulster	13
27	Dart Mountain	619	Derry	Ulster	13
28	Sawel Mountain	678	Derry	Ulster	13
29	Meenard Mountain	620	Derry	Ulster	13
30	Mullaghaneany	627	Derry	Ulster	13

Creating an adjusting report title

Because the mountains by county report is linked to a parameter query, each time we preview the report we will be asked to enter a county. The report will then display details of mountains in that county. The report is more descriptive if the report title adjusts according to the county entered. So, for example, if Sligo is entered the report title should be Mountains of Sligo, if Donegal is entered the report title should be Mountains of Donegal and so on.

1. In design view of the Mountains by County report, change the report title from 'Mountains by County' to 'Mountains of'.
2. Drag the County field from the detail section of the report and drop it to the right of the report title in the report header. Delete the label containing the text 'County' in the page header.
3. Using the format painter, copy the format from the label containing the report title to the text box containing the county field.
4. Ensure that the label and the text box are the same height. I have set the height of both to 1.1 cm (0.44 inches).
5. Position the label and text box as shown in Figure 9.4 (*for illustration purposes I have given the label a heavy border – there is no need to do this*):

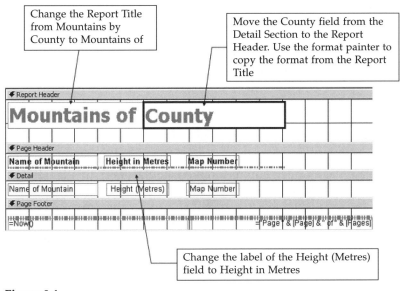

Figure 9.4

6. Preview the report and enter Sligo in the Enter Parameter Value dialogue box. Three records are displayed and the report title should appear as follows:

```
Mountains of Sligo
```

Figure 9.5

7. Preview the report again and enter Donegal. Twelve records are displayed and the report title should appear as follows:

| Mountains of Donegal |

Figure 9.6

8. Test the report by previewing it for Mayo and Derry.
9. Enter functions in the report footer to calculate the total number of mountains, the height of the highest mountain and the average mountain height. Format the functions as follows:

Number of Mountains	12
Highest Peak:	751
Average Mountain Height:	655

Figure 9.7

 (**Note:** Results displayed in Figure 9.7 are for Donegal.)

 Tip: For Access users who are also Excel users, calculating averages can cause confusion. In Access the function is =avg. In Excel the function is =average. Entering =average([Height (Metres)]) in the report footer will return an error because Access does not recognise =average as a function.

More advanced logical operators

Where data hasn't been entered in a particular field, this is referred to as a null value. Searching for null values is an important database task. For example, in a video rentals database, searching for null values in a date returned field would identify videos on rental that have not been returned. In the North West Challenge database, null values in the Date Climbed field identify mountains that have not been climbed. Searching for null values requires the **Is null** logical operator. The **Is not null** logical operator, on the other hand, can be used to find records where data **has** been entered in a particular field. In the North West Challenge database, Is not null could be used as a logical operator in the Date Climbed field to find all mountains that have been climbed.

Table 9.7

Logical Operator	*Meaning*
Is Null	Fields containing no data
Is Not Null	Fields containing data

Creating a form linked to a query

Now that details of all the mountains have been entered in the database, we can enter data in the Date Climbed and Group Members fields to complete a record each time a particular mountain is climbed. Rather than searching through all the records each time we want to enter data in the Date Climbed and Group Members fields, we will create a form linked to a query. The query will only find records where data hasn't been entered in the date climbed field and will also only display records for the particular county entered by the user. Linking a form to this query means that when you open the form, you will be asked to enter a county. The form will only display the mountains in that county which have not been climbed.

1. Create a query to find records of mountains where a date has not been entered in the Date Climbed field using *Is null* as a condition.

Field:	County	Province	Map Number	Date Climbed
Table:	600 Metre Mountains	600 Metre Mountair	600 Metre Mountair	600 Metre Mountair
Sort:				
Show:	☑	☑	☑	☑
Criteria:	[What county were you in?]			Is Null

Figure 9.8

Enter [what county were you in?] as the parameter for the county field as shown in Figure 9.8. Test the query by running it and entering Sligo. The query should find 3 records: Truskmore, Tievebaun and Cuilcagh. Save the query as **600 metre mountains not yet climbed**.

2. Create a new form linked to the 600 metre mountains not yet climbed query. Add the Name of Mountain, Height (Metres), County, Province, Date Climbed and Group Members fields. Select columnar as the form layout and expedition as the form style. The form title is **Record Trip Details.**

3. In form design select the Name of Mountain, Height (Metres), County and Province text boxes. Click the properties button and change the enabled property to no. (*This means that data cannot be entered in these fields using the Record Trip Details form.*)

4. Select all text boxes and set the font size to 12 and the font weight to bold. Set the height of all text boxes (*except for Group Members*) to 0.6 cm (0.24 inches).

5. Select all labels and set the font size to 12. Set the height of each label to 0.6 cm (0.24 inches).

6. Draw a label box in the form header and enter the text Record Trip Details. Change the font style of this label to Book Antiqua and set the font size to 28.

7. Insert clip art in the form header as shown in Figure 9.9 on page 138.

Note: You can download additional clip art to your clip gallery from www.microsoft.com.

The completed form should look something like Figure 9.9 on page 138.

Data can only be entered in the Date Climbed and Group Members text boxes because the enabled property has been set to no for all other text boxes.

	Record Trip Details		
Name of Mountain	Muckish	Height in Metres	666
County	Donegal	Province	Ulster
Date Climbed		Group Members	

Figure 9.9

Task 14 Open the record trip details form and enter Donegal in the parameter value dialog box. Scroll through the form and enter data in the Date Climbed and Group Members fields for each mountain listed in Table 9.8. (*Data has already been entered in the Name of Mountain and County fields.*)

Tip: If you have a wheel-mouse, you can quickly scroll through records by rolling the wheel with your finger.

Table 9.8

Name of Mountain	County	Date Climbed	Group Members
Muckish	Donegal	03/05/2003	Mick Byrne, Joe Doyle, Pauline Murphy, Mary Moore
Aghla Beg	Donegal	04/05/2003	Mick Byrne, Joe Doyle
Lavagh Beg	Donegal	10/05/2003	Mick Byrne, Joe Doyle, Pete Jones
Lavagh More	Donegal	10/05/2003	Mick Byrne, Joe Doyle, Pete Jones
Errigal	Donegal	17/05/2003	Mick Byrne, Joe Doyle, Pauline Murphy, Mary Moore

Close the Record Trip Details form and then open it again. Enter Donegal in the parameter value dialog box. Because the form is linked to a query that finds records of mountains where the date climbed is blank, it no longer displays details of the five mountains listed in Table 9.8. The form is now displaying 7 of the 12 mountains in Donegal. Details of all Donegal mountains can be viewed by opening the North West Mountains form.

Grouping a report

A grouped report is similar to a sorted report. However, there are a number of important differences.

- **Grouping** a report by a particular field, for example, County, lists the names of the counties in ascending alphabetical order but **each county name will appear only once in the report**.
  Sorting a report by County also lists the names of the counties in ascending alphabetical order but **each county name will appear more than once in the report.**
- Grouping a report adds an extra section, the **group header** (*grouping a report by County would add a County Header*), to the report. Data in the group header appears immediately above the records contained in each group.
- In a grouped report, calculations can be performed on data contained in each group by adding functions to the group footer. Calculations can also be performed on all of the report data by adding functions to the report footer.

Creating a grouped report

1. Using the report wizard, create a new report linked to the 600 metre Mountains Table.
2. Add the Name of Mountain, Height (Metres), County, Province and Map Number fields. Click Next.
3. To group the report by County, select County and click the single right arrow.

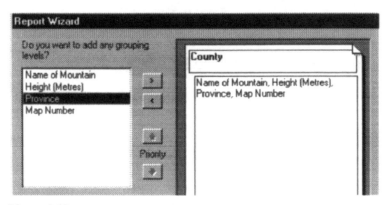

Figure 9.10

The County field appears above the other fields in the report wizard, as shown in Figure 9.10.
4. Click Next and then sort the report in ascending order of Name of Mountain.
5. Select Outline 1 as the layout, Portrait as the orientation and casual as the style in the next two steps of the report wizard.
6. Click Next and enter **North West Mountains** as the report title.
7. Click Finish to preview the report.

The name of each county appears only once in the report. This is because the report is grouped by the County field. Records associated with each county are displayed below the name of that county.

View the report design. It appears as follows:

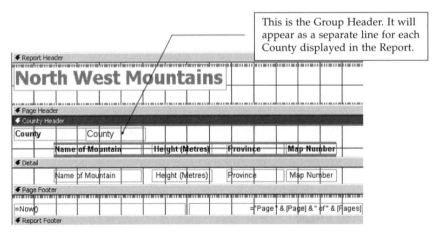

This is the Group Header. It will appear as a separate line for each County displayed in the Report.

Figure 9.11

The sections of the report (*Report Header, County Header, Detail, Page Footer*) displayed in Figure 9.11 can be seen in a preview of the report shown in Figure 9.12. This particular report doesn't have a page header.

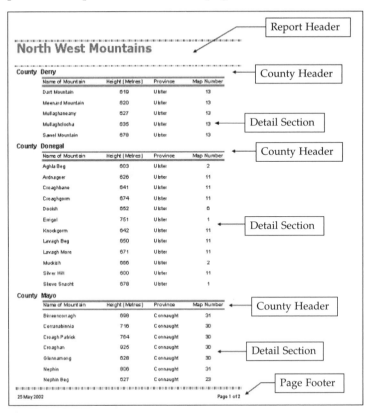

Figure 9.12

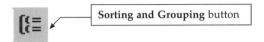

Sorting and Grouping button

Figure 9.13

The group that includes Mayo mountains is split across two pages. To stop groups from spanning across two pages, click the Sorting and Grouping button in design view of the report and change the Keep Together property of the county field from No to whole group as shown in Figure 9.14.

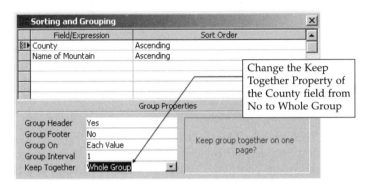

Figure 9.14

 Performing calculations on data in each group

In a grouped report, calculations can be performed on data contained in each group by adding functions to the group footer. Access does not display the group footer automatically. It can be displayed by changing the group footer property to yes in the Sorting and Grouping dialog box. Adding the function =count([name of mountain]) to the County footer results in a total of the number of mountains in each county being displayed at the end of each group: 5 in Derry, 12 in Donegal, 10 in Mayo and 3 in Sligo.

Adding the same function to the report footer has a very different effect. It returns a total of 30, which is the total for mountains in all counties.

Figure 9.15

1. In design view of the North West Mountains report, click the Sorting and Grouping button if the Sorting and Grouping dialog box is not already displayed.
2. Change the Group Footer property of the County field from No to Yes. The County Footer appears beneath the Detail section.
3. Enter the count function in the **County Footer** as shown in Figure 9.16 on page 142.
4. Preview the report. The total appears after each county.

Figure 9.16

5. Click the design view button and enter the count function in the **report footer**, as shown in Figure 9.17.

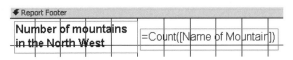

Figure 9.17

6. Preview the report again. The overall total of 30 appears on page 2, at the end of the Report.

 Task 15 Open the Record Trip Details form and enter Derry in the Parameter Value dialog box. Scroll through the form and enter data in the Date Climbed and Group Members fields for each mountain listed in Table 9.9. (*Data has already been entered in the Name of Mountain and County fields.*)

Table 9.9

Name of Mountain	County	Date Climbed	Group Members
Meenard Mountain	Derry	24/05/2003	Mick Byrne, Joe Doyle
Mullaghaneany	Derry	24/05/2003	Mick Byrne, Joe Doyle
Dart Mountain	Derry	25/05/2003	Mick Byrne, Joe Doyle, Pete Jones
Sawel Mountain	Derry	25/05/2003	Mick Byrne, Joe Doyle, Pete Jones

 **Task 16** Add functions to the North West Mountains report to calculate the number of mountains climbed in each county and the number of mountains which haven't been climbed in each county, as shown in Figure 9.18 on page 143. (**Hint:** *Calculating the total remaining requires 2 count functions.*)

You should get the answers displayed in Table 9.10 on page 143 for the remaining counties.

 Task 17 Add report functions to the **report footer** of the North West Mountains report to calculate the total number of mountains climbed to date and the number which remain, as shown in Figure 9.19 on page 143.

```
County Derry

      Name of Mountain    Height (Metres)    Province    Map Number

      Dart Mountain             619           Ulster          13

      Meenard Mountain          620           Ulster          13

      Mullaghaneany             627           Ulster          13

      Mullaghclocha             635           Ulster          13

      Sawel Mountain            678           Ulster          13

                                                   Total:  5
                                          Total Climbed:  4
                                       Total Remaining:  1
```

Figure 9.18

Table 9.10

Donegal		*Mayo*		*Sligo*	
Total	12	Total	10	Total	3
Total Climbed	5	Total Climbed	0	Total Climbed	0
Total Remaining	7	Total Remaining	10	Total Remaining	3

```
Number of mountains
  in the North West     30

      Total Climbed:      9

  Total Remaining:      21
```

Figure 9.19

Tip: Functions can be copied from one section of a report to another using copy and paste.

Note: Functions in the report footer perform calculations based on all the records in the report. Functions in the group footer perform calculations based on records in each group.

Task 18 Open the Record Trip Details form and enter Mayo in the Parameter Value dialog box. Scroll through the form and enter data in the Date Climbed and Group Members fields for each mountain listed in Table 9.11 on page 144. (*Data has already been entered in the Name of Mountain and County fields.*)

Preview the North West Mountains report. The overall total climbed is now 12 and the total remaining is 18.

Table 9.11

Name of Mountain	County	Date Climbed	Group Members
Croaghan	Mayo	30/05/2003	Mick Byrne, Joe Doyle
Slievemore	Mayo	30/05/2003	Mick Byrne, Joe Doyle
Croagh Patrick	Mayo	31/05/2003	Mick Byrne, Joe Doyle, Pauline Murphy, Mary Moore

Task 19 Create a query to find records of mountains that have not been climbed. Enter [Which county are you going to?] as the parameter for the County field. Save the query as **Plan Hill Walk**.

Note: The only difference between this query and the 600 metre mountains not yet climbed query is that each query displays a different message when it is run.

Task 20 **Display a Hillwalking Plan using a report.**

- Create a report linked to the Plan Hill Walk query. Include Name of Mountain, Height (Metres), County and Map Number fields in the report.
- Sort the report in descending order of Height (Metres).
- The report title is **Plan Hillwalking Trip**.
- Edit the report title so that it adjusts according to the county that is entered when previewing the report. Depending on which county is entered, the report title should be one of the following:
Hillwalking Plan for Derry
Hillwalking Plan for Donegal
Hillwalking Plan for Mayo
Hillwalking Plan for Sligo.
- Draw a label box in the report header immediately below the report title. Enter the text 'Displayed below is a list of mountains yet to be climbed in' in the label box.
- Drag the County field from the field list and drop to the right of this label box.
- Delete the County label and then position the county text box immediately to the right of the label box.
- Using the format painter, ensure that the label and the text box have the same formatting. This will produce an introduction to the report that will adjust depending on which county is entered when previewing the report.
- Add the count function to the report footer to calculate the number of mountains remaining to be climbed in each county.

An example of the completed report is displayed in Figure 9.20 on page 145.

Task 21 Create a query to find records of mountains that have been climbed. Save the query as **Mountains that were climbed**. (*Hint: Use Is not null to find all records where the data has been entered in the Date Climbed field.*)

```
Hillwalking Plan for Sligo

Displayed below is a list of mountains yet to
be climbed in Sligo

Name of Mountain   Height in Metres    Map Number

Cuilcagh                665               26

Truskmore               647               16

Tievebaun               611               16

                               Total:  3
```

Figure 9.20

Task 22   Create a progress report.

- Create a report linked to the Mountains that were climbed query. Include the Name of Mountain, Height (Metres), Province and County fields in the report.
- Group the report by province. Sort the report in descending order of Height (Metres).
- Select outline 1 as the layout, Portrait as the orientation and Casual as the style.
- The report title is **Progress Report**.
- Display the Province footer and enter a function that calculates the number of mountains climbed in each province.
- Insert a label box in the report header, immediately below the report title. Enter the text 'Listed below are mountains that have been climbed to date as part of the North West Challenge' in the label box. Change the style of the text to italic.
- Draw a text box in the report header to the right of the report title. Type =date() in the text box and then change the font style to Tahoma, the font size to 12 and the font weight to bold. Delete the label associated with this text box.

The completed report header, as it appears when previewed, is displayed as follows:

```
Progress Report                    31/05/2003

Listed below are the mountains which have been climbed to
date as part of the North West Challenge
```

Figure 9.21

Note: The date function displays the date from the computer's clock. The date displayed in your report will be today's date and not the date displayed in Figure 9.21, assuming the clock in your computer is correct.

Task 23   Open the Record Trip Details form and enter Sligo in the Parameter Value dialog box. Scroll through the form and enter data in the Date Climbed and Group Members fields for each mountain listed in Table 9.12 on page 146. (*Data has already been entered in the Name of Mountain and County fields.*)

Table 9.12

Name of Mountain	County	Date Climbed	Group Members
Truskmore	Sligo	08/06/2003	Mick Byrne, Joe Doyle
Tievebaun	Sligo	08/06/2003	Mick Byrne, Joe Doyle

Preview the Progress Report. The total climbed for Connaught has increased from 3 to 5.

Wildcards

In the Southside Motor Test data base, we saw that a wildcard is very useful if you are looking for field entries beginning or ending with specific characters. In relation to the Reg No field, which stored car registration numbers, we saw that using *1 as a query condition finds all registration numbers that end in 1. We also saw that using 95* as a query condition finds all registration numbers that begin with 95.

If the character or string of characters which you are looking for does not occur at the beginning or the end of the field entry, the * must be placed on either side of the character or string of characters in the query condition.

For example, finding all mountains climbed by Pauline Murphy requires a wildcard because Pauline Murphy's name is always mixed in with other names in the Group Members field. Since Pauline Murphy never occurs at the end of a field entry, *Pauline Murphy will not produce any results. Similarly, Pauline Murphy* will not produce any results because Pauline Murphy doesn't occur at the beginning of any field entry. So the correct search string is *Pauline Murphy*, which is entered in the group members field, as shown in Figure 9.22.

Field:	Group Members
Table:	600 Metre Mountains
Sort:	
Show:	☑
Criteria:	Like "*Pauline Murphy*"
or:	

Figure 9.22

Note 1: There is no need to type Like or to enclose *Pauline Murphy* in inverted commas. Access does this for you.

Note 2: *Not Like "*Pauline Murphy*"* finds all mountains that were not climbed by Pauline Murphy.

Create a separate query for each of the tasks described in Table 9.13 on page 147. Save each query using the name provided.

Table 9.13

	Purpose of Query	*Query Name*
Task 24	Find records of mountains climbed by Mary Moore	Mountains climbed by Mary Moore
Task 25	Find records of mountains climbed by Joe Doyle	Mountains climbed by Joe Doyle
Task 26	Find records of mountains that were not climbed by Pete Jones	Mountains that Pete Jones didn't climb
Task 27	Find records of mountains which have either Croagh or Knock as part of the mountain name	Mountains with Croagh or Knock in the title
Task 28	Find records of mountains in either Mayo or Derry which were climbed between 25/05/2003 and 30/05/2003 inclusive	Mayo/Derry 25/05/03 to 30/05/03
Task 29	Find records of mountains whose height is greater than or equal to 600 metres and less than 650 metres	Minor Mountains
Task 30	Find records of mountains yet to be climbed except for those in Sligo	Mountains remaining in counties other than Sligo
Task 31	Find records of mountains which are higher than 700 metres	Mountains higher than 700 metres
Task 32	Find records of mountains in Mayo or Donegal whose height is between 600 metres and 700 metres inclusive which haven't been climbed	Mayo and Donegal Mid range mountains to be climbed

Task 33 Open the Record Trip Details form and enter Mayo in the Parameter Value dialog box. Scroll through the form and enter data in the Date Climbed and Group Members fields for each mountain listed in Table 9.14. (*Data has already been entered in the Name of Mountain and County fields.*)

Table 9.14

Name of Mountain	*County*	*Date Climbed*	*Group Members*
Corranabinnia	Mayo	15/06/2003	Mick Byrne, Joe Doyle, Pauline Murphy, Mary Moore
Glennamong	Mayo	15/06/2003	Mick Byrne, Joe Doyle, Pauline Murphy, Mary Moore
Birreencoragh	Mayo	16/06/2003	Mick Byrne, Joe Doyle
Nephin	Mayo	16/06/2003	Mick Byrne, Joe Doyle

Preview the Progress Report. The total climbed for Connaught has increased from 5 to 9. Preview the Plan Hillwalking Trip report and enter Mayo in the Parameter value dialog box. Three mountains, Slieve Car, Tonacroaghaun and Nephin Beg, have not yet been climbed in Mayo.

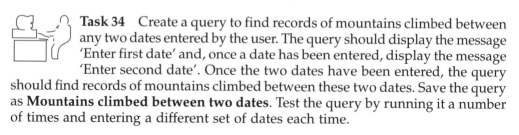

Task 34   Create a query to find records of mountains climbed between any two dates entered by the user. The query should display the message 'Enter first date' and, once a date has been entered, display the message 'Enter second date'. Once the two dates have been entered, the query should find records of mountains climbed between these two dates. Save the query as **Mountains climbed between two dates**. Test the query by running it a number of times and entering a different set of dates each time.

Task 35 Complete the database structure form (Table 9.15) with data types and field sizes for all fields in the 600 Metre Mountains table.
    Ensure that the field sizes of text fields specified in design view of the 600 Metre Mountains table match those specified in the database structure form.

Table 9.15

Field Name	Data Type	Field Size
Mountain Number		
Name of Mountain		
Height (Metres)		
County		
Province		
Map Number		
Date Climbed		
Group Members		

Toolbar buttons introduced in Assignment Nine

Datasheet View

Figure 9.23

The **Datasheet View** button: in table design click this button to see the layout of the table and to test fields.

Assignment Ten

Southern Estate Agents database

Scenario

Southern Estate Agents, based in south Dublin, is a busy estate agent specialising in the residential market. As the business grows staff are finding it more difficult to retrieve information quickly from the antiquated filing system. In Assignment Ten, you will create a database to keep track of properties that Southern Estate Agents have on offer.

Southern Estate Agents database

By completing this assignment, you will learn how to

- use the tab control in a form
- create functions in a form
- create a crosstab query
- create a crosstab report.

Task 1 Create a new database named **Southern Estate Agents**.

Task 2 Create a table with appropriate field names and data types using the sample data shown in Table 10.1 on page 150.
Set the Property Number field as the primary key. Set the default value of the Address3 field to Co. Dublin. The data type of the Highest Offer field is currency and the data type of the Date Sale Completed field is date/time. Save the table as **Property Details**. Do not enter data in the table at this point.

Tip: Set the field type for the Description field to Memo. When memo fields are used in a Form, scroll bars appear if the text entered is too long to fit in the text box.

Task 3 Create validation rules in the Property Details table as in Table 10.2 on page 150.

Table 10.1

Property Number	1
Client Firstname	Adam
Client Surname	Delaney
Address1	Beachview House
Address2	Killiney
Address3	Co. Dublin
Client Contact Number	2889876
Price	€560,000
Property Type	Semi-Detached House
No of Bedrooms	4
Parking	Yes
Alarm	Yes
Description	A substantial four bed semi-detached family residence, situated in a mature development
Highest Offer	
Date Sale Completed	

Table 10.2

Field	Purpose of Validation Rule	Validation Text
No of Bedrooms	Only allow numbers from 1 to 6 inclusive	Number of bedrooms must be in the range (1–6)
Price	Only allow numbers from 200000 to 600000 inclusive	Price must be in the range €200,000–€600,000

Using the tab control to divide a form into pages

Because there are a lot of fields in the Property Details table, arranging them all on a form would make the form appear cramped, particularly as the Description field will require a lot of space on the form. The solution is to use the tab control, which allows us to divide a form into pages.

1. Create a new form in design view, linked to the Property Details table. **N.B. Do not use the form wizard.** (*A form with no fields added is required for the tab control.*)

2. Select **View** followed by **Form Header/Footer** from the menu to add a header and footer to the form.
3. Increase the size of the Detail section of the form by dragging to the right and downwards until the form is roughly the size of the screen. Grab the bottom edge of the form footer and drag upwards so that it is not displayed.

Tab Control button

Figure 10.1

4. Click the Toolbox button if the toolbox is not already displayed and then click the Tab Control button.
5. Starting at the top left-hand corner of the Detail section, drag downwards and to the right to draw a box that occupies the entire detail section. This creates two pages in the detail section, shown in Figure 10.2. Different fields can be placed on each page and pages can be selected by clicking the page tab.

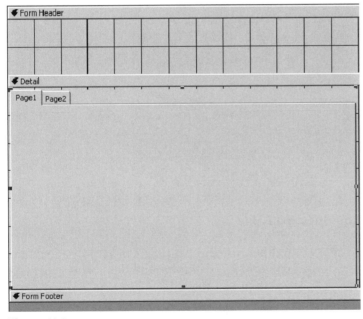

Figure 10.2

Field List button

Figure 10.3

6. Click the Field List button to display the fields in the Property Details table.
7. Drag the Property Number, Client Firstname, Client Surname, Address1, Address2, Address3, Client Contact Number, Price, Highest Offer and Date Sale Completed fields from the field list and drop them on page 1. Arrange fields and labels as shown in Figure 10.4 on page 152.

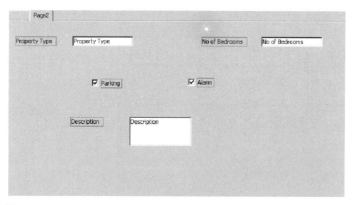

Figure 10.4

8. Click the page2 tab and add fields as shown in Figure 10.5.

Figure 10.5

9. Save the form as **Properties Available**.

Task 4   In page 1, create a combo box for the Address3 field. In page 2, create combo boxes for the Property Type and No of Bedrooms field. The values to be displayed in each combo box are shown in Table 10.3.

Table 10.3

Address3 (Combo Box)	Property Type (Combo Box)	No of Bedrooms (Combo Box)
Co. Dublin	Detached House	5
Co. Wicklow	Semi-Detached House	4
	Terraced House	3
	Apartment	2
		1

Set the limit to list property to yes for all combo boxes.

In the properties of the Property Type combo box, increase the list width to 3.8 cm (1.5 inches). This ensures that items in the combo box list are not cut off when the full list is displayed.

Task 5   We will format the Price and Highest Offer fields in a different way to the other fields so that they are given more emphasis on the form. In the label of the Price field, replace the text 'Price' with the text 'Offers in the region of'. Format the Price and Highest Offer fields as described in Table 10.4.

Table 10.4

	Price and Highest Offer Fields	
	Label	*Text Box*
Height	0.75cm (0.3 inches)	1.0 cm (0.4 inches)
Font Style	Arial	Arial
Font Colour	Navy	Red
Font Size	12	20
Font Weight	Bold	Bold
Special Effect	Flat	Flat
Back Colour	Transparent	Transparent

Set decimal places to 0 in the properties of both text boxes.

Task 6   Format all remaining labels as follows:

Table 10.5

Height	0.6 cm (0.24 inches)
Font Style	Arial
Font Colour	Black
Font Size	10
Font Weight	Bold
Special Effect	Raised

Increase the height of the labels for the Client Contact Number, Date Sale Completed and Property Type fields to 1.2 cm (0.48 inches) to allow text to wrap within these labels.

Task 7 Format all remaining text boxes as follows:

Table 10.6

Height (except for Description)	0.6 cm (0.24 inches)
Font Style	Arial
Font Colour	Navy
Font Size	12
Special Effect	Etched

Task 8 Right click the Page1 tab and select Properties. Change the Name property from Page1 to Sales Details and select the address book image as the Picture property. Display the properties of Page 2. Change the Name property from Page2 to Property Features and select the key image as the Picture property.

Task 9 Set up the form header as shown in Figure 10.6 using appropriate clip art and label boxes. (**Tip:** *Separate label boxes are needed for each line in the address.*)

Click the save button to save the changes to the Properties Available Form.

The Sales Details section of the form should look something like the following:

Figure 10.6

Task 10 In the Sales Details page, set the tab order to Property Number, Client Firstname, Client Surname, Address1, Address2, Address3, Client Contact Number, Price, Highest Offer, Date Sale Completed.

Tip: Fields will not be displayed in the tab order list unless at least one field is selected before you view the tab order.

The Property Features section of the form should look something like the following:

Figure 10.7

Task 11 In the Property Features page, set the tab order to Property Type, No of Bedrooms, Parking, Alarm, Description.

Task 12 Using the Properties Available form, enter all the records displayed in Table 10.7 on pages 156–8. Click the Property Features tab to enter data in the Property Type, No of Bedrooms, Parking, Alarm and Description fields. Data will be entered in the Highest Offer and Date Sale Completed fields at a later stage. Click the new Record Button to advance the form to each new record. When you have completed the data entry, continue with Crosstab queries below.

Crosstab queries

A crosstab query can be used to analyse a table where data is repeated in two or more fields. In the Property Details table (Table 10.7), data is repeated in the Address2 field (Killiney occurs twice, Shankill occurs three times etc.) and the Property Type field. (Apartment occurs three times, detached house occurs three times etc.)

In the crosstab query these fields are organised so that the data items that are repeated become row and column headings. In the example in Table 10.8 on page 159, the column headings are generated by the Property Type field and the row headings are generated by the Address2 field.

Once the structure of the crosstab query is established, we can perform a calculation on a selected field for each cell in the grid where data occurs. For example, if we

Table 10.7

Property Number	Client First-name	Client Surname	Address1	Address2	Address3	Client Contact Number	Price	Property Type	No of Bedrooms	Parking	Alarm	Description
1	Adam	Delaney	Beachview House	Killiney	Co. Dublin	2889876	€ 560,000	Semi-Detached House	4	Yes	Yes	A substantial four bed semi-detached family residence, situated in a mature development
2	Joan	Murphy	3 Corbawn Terrace	Shankill	Co. Dublin	2986017	€ 247,500	Semi-Detached House	3	Yes	No	Extensive range of kitchen floor and wall units
3	Pauline	Byrne	23 Seaview Park	Dun Laoghaire	Co. Dublin	2883011	€ 280,000	Semi-Detached House	3	Yes	No	A spacious semi-detached 3-bedroom property situated in a quiet cul-de-sac
4	Daniel	Murphy	Rose Lawn	Sandycove	Co. Dublin	2786581	€ 380,000	Terraced House	2	No	No	Rare opportunity to purchase this well-presented 2-bedroom terraced house retaining many of its original features
5	Peter	Looney	16 Wolverton Grove	Shankill	Co. Dublin	2685509	€ 343,000	Detached House	4	Yes	Yes	No. 16 boasts excellent gardens to front and rear, and a wonderful sunny westerly orientation
6	Carl	O Donnell	4 Martello Road	Dalkey	Co. Dublin	2785002	€ 255,000	Terraced House	2	No	No	This is an impressive cottage of immense character situated in a quiet cul-de-sac

(Contd)

Table 10.7 (*Contd*)

Property Number	Client First-name	Client Surname	Address1	Address2	Address3	Client Contact Number	Price	Property Type	No of Bedrooms	Parking	Alarm	Description
7	Fiona	Stapleton	27 Abbey Lane	Dun Laoghaire	Co. Dublin	2581162	€325,000	Apartment	1	Yes	No	Superbly positioned ground floor 1 bedroom apartment offering superior space and an imaginative design
8	Tadhg	Donovan	12 Bayview Mews	Glasthule	Co. Dublin	2682297	€295,000	Semi-Detached House	3	Yes	No	A truly delightful modern family home presented with impeccable taste in this much sought after development
9	Jack	Dunne	1 Richmond Close	Killiney	Co. Dublin	2584029	€280,000	Apartment	2	Yes	No	Spacious modern apartment with parking
10	Ian	Mc Shane	3 Eden Terrace	Monks-town	Co. Dublin	2789942	€255,000	Terraced House	2	No	No	Ideally located brick-built town residence situated in a quiet mews laneway
11	Philip	Donovan	28 Rockford Manor	Bray	Co. Wicklow	2480002	€247,500	Semi-Detached House	3	Yes	Yes	Situated in a quiet cul-de-sac, the property is within walking distance of Bray Shopping Centre
12	Gerry	O Neill	28 Dorney Road	Dun Laoghaire	Co. Dublin	2889783	€245,000	Semi-Detached House	3	Yes	No	A most attractive and exclusive residential property

Table 10.7 *(Contd)*

Property Number	Client First-name	Client Surname	Address1	Address2	Address3	Client Contact Number	Price	Property Type	No of Bedrooms	Parking	Alarm	Description
13	Anthony	Murphy	136 O Flynn Park	Bray	Co. Wicklow	2788850	€ 245,000	Semi-Detached House	3	Yes	Yes	A wonderfully presented family home located in this quiet, extremely attractive modern development
14	Roisin	Murray	122 Plunkett Road	Shankill	Co. Dublin	2781010	€ 220,000	Terraced House	3	No	No	Modern mid-terrace brick-fronted townhouse
15	Garreth	Moore	46 Ashlawn Grove	Stillorgan	Co. Dublin	2786033	€ 205,000	Terraced House	3	Yes	Yes	Conveniently situated within a stroll of shops and all amenities
16	Geraldine	Walsh	38 Seaview Court	Stillorgan	Co. Dublin	2682912	€ 315,000	Apartment	2	No	No	No. 38 is a garden-level 2-bed apartment within a large period building
17	Paul	Mc Carthy	22 Anville Wood	Dun Laoghaire	Co. Dublin	2281994	€ 520,000	Detached House	5	Yes	Yes	Exceptionally spacious 5-bedroom detached family home
18	Andrew	Collins	101 Westgrove	Glasthule	Co. Dublin	2283076	€ 485,000	Detached House	4	Yes	Yes	Tucked away in this quiet, mature cul-de-sac development lies this deceptively spacious family home with a wonderfully sunny southerly rear garden
19	Neill	Conlon	28 Millwood Downs	Bray	Co. Wicklow	2086789	€ 415,000	Semi-Detached House	4	Yes	Yes	Superbly renovated 4-bedroom home with sea views
20	Tommy	Dunne	7 Allen Park Road	Dalkey	Co. Dublin	2282055	€ 370,000	Semi-Detached House	3	Yes	Yes	Boasting superb landscaped gardens, this is a most attractive 3-bedroom semi-detached family residence

selected the property number as the field and count as the calculation, the number of apartments, detached houses, semi-detached houses and terraced houses in each location would be calculated, as displayed as in Table 10.9.

Table 10.8

	Apartment	Detached House	Semi-Detached House	Terraced House
Bray				
Dalkey				
Dun Laoghaire				
Glasthule				
Killiney				
Monkstown				
Sandycove				
Shankill				
Stillorgan				

Table 10.9

	Apartment	Detached House	Semi-Detached House	Terraced House
Bray			3	
Dalkey			1	1
Dun Laoghaire	1	1	2	
Glasthule		1	1	
Killiney	1		1	
Monkstown				1
Sandycove				1
Shankill		1	1	1
Stillorgan	1			1

Not all cells in the grid contain data. For example, there are no apartments, detached houses or terraced houses available in Bray so these cells are empty in the first row. From the results of the crosstab query, it can be quickly seen that there are 3 semi-detached houses in Bray, 1 semi-detached house and 1 terraced house in Dalkey and so on. Adding all the numbers gives 20, which is the number of records stored in the Property Details table (Table 10.7).

Conditions can be added to a crosstab query so that summary totals are calculated for specific records. If, for example, we added a condition so that records are only displayed where the price is €250,000 or less, we would get the following results:

Table 10.10

	Semi-Detached House	*Terraced House*
Bray	1	
Bray	1	
Dun Laoghaire	1	
Shankill		1
Shankill	1	
Stillorgan		1

Creating a crosstab query

In the following example, we will create a crosstab query to analyse the number of apartments, detached houses, semi-detached houses and terraced houses available in each location.

1. In the database window, select queries, click new, select crosstab query wizard and then click OK.
2. The Property Details table is highlighted indicating it contains the fields for the query. Click next.
3. Add Address2 to the selected fields box. This will generate row headings from the Address2 field. Click Next.
4. Select Property Type as the column heading. This will generate column headings from the Property Type field. Click Next.
5. Select Property Number as the calculated field and Count as the function. Click Next.
6. Enter **Analysis of Market Supply** as the query name.
7. Click Finish to view the results of the query.

Task 13 Create a crosstab query that calculates the average price for each Property Type in each Location. Save the query as **Average price of property types by area**. (*Notice that the price displayed for a semi-detached house in Dun Laoghaire is €262,500. This is the average of the two semi-detached houses available in Dun Laoghaire – €280,000+€245,000 divided by 2 = €262,500.*)

Task 14 Create a crosstab query that displays the highest price for each Property Type in each Location. Save the query as **Highest prices of property types by area**.

Task 15 Create a crosstab query that displays the lowest price for each Property Type in each location. Save the query as **Lowest prices of property types by area**.

Displaying the results of a crosstab query using a report

In the following example, we will create a report to display the results of the Analysis of market supply crosstab query.

1. Using the report wizard, create a new report linked to the Analysis of market supply query.
2. Add all fields except for Total of Property Number.
3. Skip grouping. Sort the report in ascending order of Address2.
4. Select Tabular as the layout, Portrait as the orientation and Corporate as the style.
5. Enter **Market Supply Report** as the title. Click Finish to preview the report.
6. In report design, edit the Address2 label so that it reads Property Location.
7. Select the labels and text boxes for each Property Type and click the center button.
8. In the report footer, enter functions to calculate the total number of properties available in each category. (*=sum([Apartment]) calculates the total number of apartments available. =sum([Detached House]) calculates the total number of detached houses available. A separate function is required for each property type.*)
9. Copy the address and logo from the form header of the properties available form and paste into the report header.
   The completed report should appear as shown in Figure 10.8.

Market Supply Report				Southern Estate Agents 1 Main Street, Ballybrack, Tel: (01)667 9923	
Property Location	Apartment	Detached House	Semi-Detached House	Terraced House	
Bray			3		
Dalkey			1	1	
Dun Laoghaire	1	1	2		
Glasthule		1	1		
Killiney	1		1		
Monkstown				1	
Sandycove				1	
Shankill		1	1	1	
Stillorgan	1			1	
Total:	**3**	**3**	**9**	**5**	

Figure 10.8

Fill/Back Colour button

Figure 10.9

Tip: The area containing the calculations can be shaded by selecting the report footer in report design, clicking the Fill/Back Colour button and then selecting light grey from the colour palette.

10. Print the Market Supply report.

Task 16   Display highest prices of property types using a report.

• Create a report linked to the Highest prices of property types by area query. Include all fields except for Total of Price in the report.
• Sort the report in ascending order of Address2.
• The report title is **Highest Prices of Property Types by Area**.
• Add functions to the report footer to display the highest price of each property type.
• Format all functions so that the results are displayed in currency format without decimal places.

Task 17   Display lowest prices of property types using a report.

• Create a report linked to the Lowest prices of property types by area query. Include all fields except for Total of Price in the report.
• Sort the report in ascending order of Address2.
• The report title is **Lowest Prices of Property Types by Area**.
• Add functions to the report footer to display the lowest price of each property type.
• Format all functions so that the results are displayed in currency format without decimal places.

Task 18   Create a query to find records of properties currently on the market. Save the query as Properties for Sale. (Hint: *Use the logical operator Is null.*)

Task 19   Display properties currently on the market using a report.

• Create a report linked to the Properties for sale query. Include the Address1, Address2, Address3, Price, Property type and No of Bedrooms fields in the report.
• Group the report by Address2 and sort the report in descending order of Price.
• Select Align Left 1 as the layout, Portrait as the orientation and Corporate as the style.
• The report title is **Properties Currently on the Market**.

- Copy the address and logo from the Properties Available form to the report header.
- Insert a function in the report header to count the number of records in the report. Combine this function with a label so that it appears as '20 properties available'
- Draw a label immediately below this and enter the text 'Please phone the office for a viewing time'.
- Display the Address2 footer and insert a function to calculate the average price of a property in each area.
- Delete the labels and the horizontal line in the Address2 header as shown in the extract from the report (Figure 10.10).
- Print the Properties Currently on the market report.

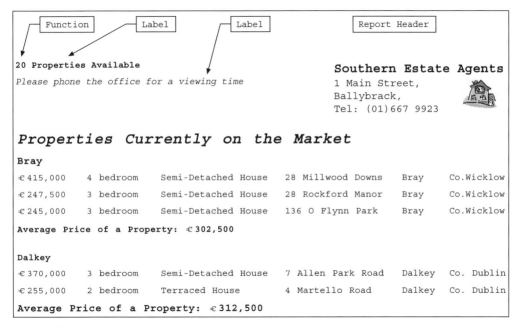

Figure 10.10

 Tip: The word 'bedroom' is inserted in a label between the No of Bedrooms field and the Property Type field in the Detail section of the report.

 Task 20 Create a parameter query which displays the message 'Enter preferred location of property' when it is run. The query should find records of properties that haven't been sold in the location entered by the user. Save the query as **Properties by location**. Test the query by running it and entering Shankill as the location. Three records should be displayed.

Task 21 Display records of properties matching the location entered.

- Create a report linked to the Properties by location query. Include the Price, No of Bedrooms, Property Type, Address1, Address2 and Address3 fields in the report.
- Sort the report in ascending order of Price.
- Format the report as shown in Figure 10.11. Use labels, text boxes and clip art in the report header as in Task 19.
- Save the report as **Properties for Sale by Location**.

Displayed in Figure 10.11 is the output of the report having entered Dun Laoghaire in the parameter value dialog box.

```
4  Properties  Available                Southern Estate Agents
                                        1 Main Street,
                                        Ballybrack,
                                        Tel: (01)667 9923


Properties for Sale in Dun Laoghaire

Price        Property Type                           Address
─────────────────────────────────────────────────────────────────────────
€ 245,000    3 bedroom  Semi-Detached House   28 Dorney Road   Dun Laoghaire  Co.Dublin

€ 280,000    3 bedroom  Semi-Detached House   23 Seaview Park  Dun Laoghaire  Co.Dublin

€ 325,000    1 bedroom  Apartment             27 Abbey Lane    Dun Laoghaire  Co.Dublin

€ 520,000    5 bedroom  Detached House        22 Anville Wood  Dun Laoghaire  Co.Dublin
```

Figure 10.11

Tip: To create a report title that adjusts according to the location entered in the parameter value dialog box requires a label and the Address2 text box in the report header. The Address2 field can be dragged from the field list and dropped in the report header.

Test the report by previewing it a number of times, entering a different location each time.

Task 22 Open the Properties Available form. Scroll through the records to find each property displayed in Table 10.11 and enter data in the Highest Offer and Date Sale completed fields. (*Data has already been entered in the Property Number and Address fields.*)

Table 10.11

Property Number	Address1	Address2	Address3	Highest Offer	Date Sale Completed
2	3 Corbawn Terrace	Shankill	Co. Dublin	€250,000	09/05/2003
13	136 O Flynn Park	Bray	Co. Wicklow	€243,500	21/05/2003
17	22 Anville Wood	Dun Laoghaire	Co. Dublin	€500,000	29/05/2003

Tip: If you have a wheel-mouse, you can quickly scroll through records by rolling the wheel with your finger.

Adding a function to the form header

In design view of the Properties Available form, draw a text box in the form header to the left of the title. Enter =count([Property Number]) in the text box and then delete the label attached to the text box. This function counts the number of records displayed by the form. Click the form view button to view the records. The form title should now be '20 Properties Available'. This is not accurate because three properties have just been sold. To ensure that the form does not display records of properties that have been sold, link the form to the Properties for Sale query by viewing the properties of the form, and changing the record source of the form to Properties for Sale. Click the form view button. The form title should now appear as displayed in Figure 10.12.

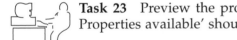

Figure 10.12

Task 23 Preview the properties currently on the market report. '17 Properties available' should be displayed in the report header.

Task 24 Create a parameter query which displays the message 'Enter the maximum the customer can afford' when it is run. The query should find records of properties *which haven't been sold* where the price is less than or equal to the number entered. Save the query as **Properties in a customers price range**. Test the query by running it and entering 220000 as the maximum. Two records should be displayed.

Task 25 **Display property search results using a report.**

- Create a report linked to the Properties in a customer's price range query. Include the Address1, Address2, Address3, No of bedrooms, Property Type and Price fields in the report.
- Sort the report in ascending order of Price.
- Create a report title that adjusts according to the number of records displayed in the report. If 5 records are displayed in the report, the title should be '5 properties matched your search'. If ten records are displayed in the report, the title should be '10 properties matched your search', and so on.
- Test the report by previewing it and entering 250000 as the maximum the customer can afford.

The report should appear displayed in Figure 10.13.

---

4 Properties Matched Your Search

Price	Property Type	Address		
€ 205,000	3 bedroom Terraced House	46 Ashlawn Grove	Stillorgan	Co.Dublin
€ 220,000	3 bedroom Terraced House	122 Plunkett Road	Shankill	Co.Dublin
€ 245,000	3 bedroom Semi-Detached House	28 Dorney Road	Dun Laoghaire	Co.Dublin
€ 247,500	3 bedroom Semi-Detached House	28 Rockford Manor	Bray	Co.Wicklow

Figure 10.13

Save the report as **Properties by Price**.

Task 26   Open the Properties Available form. Scroll through the records to find each property displayed in Table 10.12 and enter data in the Highest Offer and Date Sale Completed fields. (*Data has already been entered in the property number and address fields.*)

Table 10.12

Property Number	Address1	Address2	Address3	Highest Offer	Date Sale Completed
15	46 Ashlawn Grove	Stillorgan	Co. Dublin	€207,000	06/06/2003
6	4 Martello Road	Dalkey	Co. Dublin	€255,000	11/06/2003
20	7 Allen Park Road	Dalkey	Co. Dublin	€375,000	17/06/2003
5	16 Wolverton Grove	Shankill	Co. Dublin	€350,000	27/06/2003

   Close the form and preview the Properties Currently on the Market report. There should be 13 Properties available. Open the Properties available form again. The form header should display 13 Properties Available.

Task 27   Create a query to find records of properties which have been sold. (**Hint:** *Use Is not null.*) Save the query as **Completed Sales**.

Task 28   Create a sales report.

   • Create a report linked to the Completed Sales query. Include the Price, No of Bedrooms, Property Type, Address1, Address2, Address3 and Date Sale Completed fields in the report.
• Group the report by Date Sale Completed.

- Sort the report in ascending order of Address2.
- Select Align Left 1 as the layout, portrait as the orientation and Corporate as the style.
- The report title is **Sales Report**.
- Display the Date Sale Completed footer and add functions to calculate the number of properties sold per month and the total monthly sales revenue.
- Add functions to the report footer to calculate the total sales revenue for the period, the average price received for a property and the total number of properties sold.
- Format the report as shown in Figure 10.14.

	Southern Estate Agents
Sales Report	1 Main Street, Ballybrack, Tel: (01) 667 9923

May 2003

Price	Property Type	Address	
€245,000	3 bedroom Semi-Detached House	136 O Flynn Park Bray	Co. Wicklow
€520,000	5 bedroom Detached House	22 Anville Wood Dun Laoghaire	Co. Dublin
€247,500	3 bedroom Semi-Detached House	3 Corbawn Terrace Shankill	Co. Dublin

Number of properties sold:	3
Total Sales Revenue:	€1,012,500

June 2003

Price	Property Type	Address	
€370,000	3 bedroom Semi-Detached House	7 Allen Park Road Dalkey	Co. Dublin
€255,000	2 bedroom Terraced House	4 Martello Road Dalkey	Co. Dublin
€343,000	4 bedroom Detached House	16 Wolverton Grove Shankill	Co. Dublin
€205,000	3 bedroom Terraced House	45 Ashlawn Grove Stillorgan	Co. Dublin

Number of properties Sold:	4
Total Sales Revenue:	€1,173,000

Report Summary

Total sales revenue for the period:	€2,185,500
Average price received for a property:	€312,214
Number of completed sales:	7

Figure 10.14

Task 29 Create the letter displayed below using Microsoft Word. **(Don't type the field names, displayed in bold print.)**

<<Client_Firstname>> <<Client_Surname>>   Southern Estate Agents
<<Address1>>   1 Main Street,
<<Address2>>   Ballybrack,
<<Address3>>   Tel: (01)667 9923

Dear <<Client_Firstname>>,

We are pleased to inform you that the sale of your property was completed on <<Date_Sale_Completed>>. The highest offer on your property was <<Highest_Offer>> and the sale will now be concluded at this price. Please contact your solicitor for details of contracts to be signed and the closing date of the sale.

   It only remains for us to thank you for choosing Southern Estate Agents and to wish you all the best with your new property.

Yours sincerely,

_____

Adam Doodle
Managing Director

Save the letter as **Completed Sale Notification.**.

Using the Mail Merge facility set this letter up as a main document. Use the completed sales query as the data source and insert fields from the database, shown in bold print above.

 Tip: Before implementing the Mail Merge, ensure that decimal places is set to 0 for the Price field in the Property Details table.

 Task 30   Merge the main document with the data source to produce a new document containing seven letters. Save this document as **Sales Notifications for June and July**.

Task 31   In Microsoft Access, use the label wizard to produce labels for all clients receiving letters. Each label should have the Client Firstname, Client Surname, Address1, Address2 and Address3 fields and should be set up as shown in Table 10.13. Sort the labels in ascending order of Client Surname. The report name is **Labels for sales completed in June and July**. Print the labels either on an A4 page or on a sheet of laser labels.

   Create a separate query for each of the tasks described in Table 10.14. Save each query using the name provided. Print the results of each query in landscape orientation.

 Task 41   Complete the database structure form (Table 10.15) with data types and field sizes for all fields in the Property Details table.

Table 10.13

> Tommy Dunne
> 7 Allen Park Road
> Dalkey
> Co. Dublin

Table 10.14

	Purpose of Query	*Query Name*
Task 32	Find records of available properties costing €300,000 or less	Properties for €300,000 or less
Task 33	Find records of available properties where the price is greater than €300,000 and less than €500,000	Properties between €300,000 and €500,000
Task 34	Find records of available properties costing €500,000 or more	Properties for €500,000 or more
Task 35	Find records of available semi-detached properties with 3 or more bedrooms with both parking and an alarm	Semi-detached 3+ bedrooms, parking and alarm
Task 36	Find records of available properties in Dun Laoghaire or Sandycove costing between €300,000 and €500,000 inclusive	Dun Laoghaire/Sandycove between €300,000 and €500,000
Task 37	Find records of available semi-detached properties costing less than €300,000	Semi-detached properties under €300,000
Task 38	Find records of terraced and semi-detached properties available in Dun Laoghaire, Sandycove and Monkstown	Terraced/Semi-detached in Dun Laoghaire, Sandycove and Monkstown
Task 39	Find records of available properties where the garden is a feature	Properties with featured garden
Task 40	Find records of available properties with sea views	Properties with sea views

Ensure that the field sizes of text fields specified in design view of the Property Details table match those specified in the database structure form.

Table 10.15

Field Name	Data Type	Field Size
Property Number		
Client Firstname		
Client Surname		
Address1		
Address2		
Address3		
Client Contact Number		
Price		
Property Type		
No of Bedrooms		
Parking		
Alarm		
Description		
Highest Offer		
Date Sale Completed		

Toolbar buttons introduced in Assignment Ten

Figure 10.15

The **Tab Control button:** to divide a form into pages, click this button in form design and drag to draw a box in the detail section.

Figure 10.16

The **Fill/Back Colour button:** in form design or report design click this button to colour the background of a selected label or text box. The fill/back colour button can also be used to colour in a section of a form or report.

Important buttons to remember

Figure 10.17

The **Field List button:** in form design or report design click this button to see the list of fields included in the table or query which the form/report is linked to.

Progress test 3

Complete the test by writing answers in the space provided or by circling the correct answer for each question.

1. Which of the following buttons is used to create a text box?

   a.

   Figure 10.18

   b.

   Figure 10.19

   c.

   Figure 10.20

   d.

   Figure 10.21

2. Complete the following table by entering the storage size in bytes required for each data type:

Table 10.16

Number Type	Storage Size (bytes)
Autonumber	
Date/Time	
Yes/No	
Currency	

3. Fill in the blanks:

Implementing a Mail Merge requires the following steps:

a. Create the _____ using Microsoft Word

b. Identify the _____

c. Insert the _____ fields in the _____

d. Merge the _____ with the _____

4. In Table 10.17, describe where each report section appears in a printed report.

Table 10.17

Report Section	Appears
Report Header	
Page Header	
Group Header	
Detail	
Group Footer	
Page Footer	
Report Footer	

5. Displayed is an extract from the design of a report.

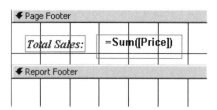

Figure 10.22

When the report is previewed, the sum function returns an error. What is the reason for this?

6. The codes displayed in Table 10.18 are stored in a field named Code whose data type is text:

Table 10.18

Code
144285-OEM-0009123-93456
144285-OEM-0009123-93457
144285-OEM-0009123-93458
244285-OEX-0009123-93456
244285-OEX-0009123-93457
244285-OEX-0009123-93458

Complete Table 10.19 by entering search strings required to find the data indicated.

Table 10.19

Search For	Query Search String required in Code field
All codes beginning with 1	
All codes beginning with 2	
All codes ending in 6	
All codes containing the letters OEM	
All codes containing the letters OEX	

7. In order for a calculation to be repeated a number of times in a report, a function must be created in the

    a. report header
    b. group footer
    c. report footer

8. Complete Table 10.20 by entering the meaning of each logical operator.

Table 10.20

Logical Operator	Meaning
Is Null	
Is Not Null	

9. Validation rules are normally entered in

    a. table design
    b. form design
    c. query design
    d. report design

10. Which of the following buttons is used to view the properties of an object?

    a.

    Figure 10.23

b.

Figure 10.24

c.

Figure 10.25

d.

Figure 10.26

SECTION 4

Introduction to Relational Database

Assignment Eleven

Exam Management System database

Assignment Eleven

Exam Management System database

Scenario

Ann Mitchell runs a busy Information Technology College in Cork. Recently, she has been finding it increasingly difficult to keep track of all the administration work generated by exams, which happen twice yearly. In Assignment Eleven you will create a relational database application to manage the administration of student exams.

Exam Management System database

By completing this assignment, you will learn how to

- create a database containing multiple tables
- set up relationships between tables
- create a combo box linked to a table
- create a form linked to multiple tables
- create a macro to speed up data entry
- develop custom database menus
- create a query linked to another query
- create an update query.

This assignment is designed to introduce you to the concepts and practical applications of relational databases. It is not meant to be a comprehensive guide to relational databases. For this reason, I have placed less emphasis on explanation and more emphasis on learning by doing.

What is a relational database?

So far we have created databases where all the records are stored in one table. In a relational database the records are stored in two or more tables. Consequently, queries can find data in multiple tables and reports can display data from multiple tables. In a relational database, a form can enter data in one table while displaying data from other tables.

Task 1 Create a new database named **Exam Management System**.

Tip: Relational databases require more disk storage space. By the time you have completed this assignment, the Exam Management System database will be too big to fit on a floppy disk. For this reason, it is advisable to store it on a hard disk or zip disk from the beginning.

Task 2 Create a table to store data relating to **mentors** with appropriate field names and data types using the sample data shown in Table 11.1.

Table 11.1

Mentor Code	RLQN
Mentor Name	Rachel Quinn
Extension Number	2185

Set the Mentor Code field as the primary key. **Save the table as Mentors**. Do not enter data in the table at this point.

Task 3 Create a table to store data relating to **students** with appropriate field names and data types using the sample data shown in Table 11.2.

Table 11.2

Student Code	03CP001
Firstname	Domnic
Surname	Brennan
Address1	The Heath
Address2	Fermoy
Address3	Co. Cork
Course	Computer Programming
Start Date	01/09/2003
Finish Date	
Certificate	No
Mentor Code	RLQN

Set the Student Code field as the primary key. Save the table as **Students**. Do not enter data in the table at this point.

Linking the Mentors table and the Students table

Each mentor is responsible for a group of students. Each student has only one mentor. The mentor code RLQN can only be entered once in the mentors table because Mentor Code is the primary key but it can be entered in the students table many times depending on how many students Rachel Quinn is responsible for. This is called a one-to-many relationship.

Referential integrity

Referential integrity is a system used by Access to ensure that data in related tables follows the rules of the one-to-many relationship and that data is not accidentally deleted. Referential integrity can be enforced as long as the linking fields have the same data type and one of the linking fields is the primary key.

Enforcing referential integrity means that

1. a Mentor Code cannot be entered in the Mentor Code field in the Students table unless that code already exists in the Mentors table
2. the entire record of a particular mentor cannot be deleted from the Mentors table while there are references to the Mentor Code of that mentor in the Students table.
3. the Mentor Code cannot be altered in the Mentors table while there are references to that Mentor Code in the Students table.

Figure 11.1

To set up the relationship between the Mentors table and the Students table click the relationships button. Add the Mentors table and then add the Students table. Close the show table dialog box. A one-to-many relationship is set up by dragging the primary key from the table on the one side of the relationship (*Mentor Code in the Mentors table*) to the related field in the table on the many side of the relationship (*Mentor Code in the Students table*).

Drag the Mentor Code field from the Mentors table and drop on the Mentor Code field in the Students table. In the edit relationships box, click the Enforce Referential Integrity box. Notice that Access shows the relationship type as one-to-many.

Tip: Access will not set up the relationship unless the linking fields have the same data type. In this case Mentor Code should be given a data type of text and a field size of 4 in both tables.

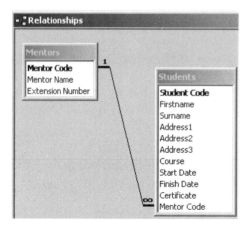

Figure 11.2

(**Note:**   *The sideways 8 is the mathematical symbol for infinity.*)

Task 4   Create a form linked to the Mentors table. A suggested layout and format for the form is shown in Figure 11.3.

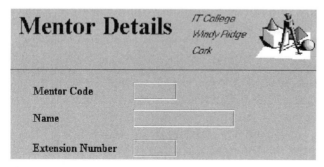

Figure 11.3

Save the form as **Mentor Details**.

At this stage, I will leave it up to you to decide on an appropriate format for the form. As we will use a number of different forms in this assignment, once you have decided on a format, you should apply that format to all forms.

Task 5   Using the Mentor Details form, enter all the records shown in Table 11.3.

Creating the student details form

Each time a new student is entered in the database, we also enter the code for his or her mentor. We will create a combo box to enter the Mentor Codes

Table 11.3

Mentor Code	Mentor Name	Extension Number
BNSN	Brian Sullivan	2973
JNAG	Jane Armstrong	2601
PRRY	Peter Reilly	2098
RLQN	Rachel Quinn	2185

but instead of typing in the values for the combo box, we will set it up so that the combo box looks for the Mentor Codes in the Mentors table.

1. Create a new form linked to the Students table. Add all fields except for Finish Date and Certificate.
2. Create a combo box for the Course field. (*Ensure that the control wizard is on.*) The values to be displayed in the combo box are shown in Table 11.4.

Table 11.4

Course (Combo Box)
Computer Programming
Information Technology
Web Design

3. Set the limit to list property of the combo box to yes.
4. Create a combo box for the Mentor Code field. Select 'I want the combo box to look up the values in a table or query' and click Next.
5. Select the Mentors table and click Next.
6. Add Mentor Code and Mentor Name to the combo box and click Next.
7. Ensure that the Hide Key Column box is ticked. Click Next.
8. Store the value in the Mentor Code field. Click Next.
9. Enter Mentor as the label for the combo box. Click Finish.
10. Set the tab order of the form to Student Code, Firstname, Surname, Address1, Address2, Address3, Course, Start Date, Mentor Code. A suggested layout and format for the form is shown in Figure 11.4.
11. Save the form as **Student Registration**.

 Task 6 Using the Student Registration form, enter all the records displayed in Table 11.5 on page 183.

Figure 11.4

Note 1: Selecting Rachel Quinn in the Mentor Code combo box results in the code RLQN being entered in the Mentor Code field in the Students table. This is also the case for the other mentor codes.

Note 2: There are two students named John Murphy in the students table. The primary key will be used to ensure the 'correct John Murphy' is selected as the matter arises.

When you have entered all the data, open the Students table in the datasheet view. Notice that the four character codes have been entered in the Mentor Code field even though we selected the mentor names from the combo box.

Task 7 Create a report that lists students by course.

- Using the report wizard, create a new report linked to the Students table.
- Add the Firstname, Surname and Course fields.
- Group the report by Course.
- Sort the report in ascending order of Surname.
- Select an appropriate layout, orientation. Select Corporate as the report style. The report title is **List of Current Students**.
- Add a function to calculate the total number of students in each course.

Task 8 Create a report that lists students by mentor.
Because this report will display fields from the Students table and the Mentors table, a query containing fields from both tables must firstly be created. The report will be linked to this query.

- Create a new query and add both the Mentors table and Students table. From the Mentors table add the Mentor Name field to the query design grid. From the Students table add the Firstname, Surname and Course fields to the query design grid. Click the Run button to view the data found by the query. Data from both tables is displayed. This data will be used by the report. Save the query as **Mentors and Students**.

Table 11.5

Student Code	Firstname	Surname	Address1	Address2	Address3	Course	Start Date	Mentor
03CP001	Domnic	Brennan	The Heath	Fermoy	Co. Cork	Computer Programming	01/09/2003	Rachel Quinn
03CP002	Brendan	Dunne	87 Earlsfort Mews	Ballinlough	Cork	Computer Programming	01/09/2003	Peter Reilly
03CP003	Tadhg	Scanlan	9 Woodvale Grove	Rochestown	Co. Cork	Computer Programming	01/09/2003	Jane Armstrong
03CP004	Diarmuid	Scott	82 Glendale Park	Clogheen	Co. Tipperary	Computer Programming	01/09/2003	Jane Armstrong
03CP005	Rod	Hogan	The Elms	Ballinlough	Cork	Computer Programming	01/09/2003	Brian Sullivan
03IT001	Maura	Clohosey	31 Hillcourt Park	Killarney	Co. Kerry	Information Technology	08/09/2003	Rachel Quinn
03IT002	Tony	Gallagher	20 Glenbourne Close	Rochestown	Co. Cork	Information Technology	08/09/2003	Rachel Quinn
03IT003	Michael	O Neill	15 Newgrove Avenue	Blackrock	Cork	Information Technology	08/09/2003	Peter Reilly
03IT004	John	Murphy	Woodhaven	Kenmare	Co. Kerry	Information Technology	08/09/2003	Brian Sullivan
03IT005	Deirdre	Moroney	26 Charleville Court	Tralee	Co. Kerry	Information Technology	08/09/2003	Peter Reilly
03IT006	Colin	Evans	The Hollows	Mallow	Co. Cork	Information Technology	08/09/2003	Jane Armstrong
03IT007	Eamonn	Twomey	1 Castlefield Court	Douglas	Cork	Information Technology	08/09/2003	Jane Armstrong
03IT008	Nora	Sheehan	Glenview	Ballinlough	Cork	Information Technology	08/09/2003	Jane Armstrong
03IT009	Susan	Wright	Hillcrest Manor	Glasheen	Cork	Information Technology	08/09/2003	Brian Sullivan
03IT010	Sean	Noonan	13 Eden Park Drive	Douglas	Cork	Information Technology	08/09/2003	Brian Sullivan
03WD001	Ciara	Mooney	48 Auburn Road	Douglas	Cork	Web Design	15/09/2003	Rachel Quinn
03WD002	Robin	Carr	6 Springlawn Park	Dungarvan	Co. Waterford	Web Design	15/09/2003	Rachel Quinn
03WD003	Elaine	Mc Carthy	3 Cairnwood Grove	Raheen	Limerick	Web Design	15/09/2003	Peter Reilly
03WD004	Paula	King	4 Fairview Heights	Macroom	Co. Cork	Web Design	15/09/2003	Brian Sullivan
03WD005	John	Murphy	8 Old Court Road	Douglas	Cork	Web Design	15/09/2003	Peter Reilly

- Using the report wizard, create a new report linked to the Mentors and Students query. Add all fields to the report.
- Group the report by Mentor Name.
- Sort the report in ascending order of Surname.
- Select an appropriate layout and orientation. Select Corporate as the report style. The report title is **Mentor Groups**.
- Adjust the design of the report so that data appears in the Mentor Name header as follows:
  Mentor: Brian Sullivan
  Mentor: Jane Armstrong
  Mentor: Peter Reilly
  Mentor: Rachel Quinn
- Add a function to calculate the total number of students in each group.

Task 9   Create a table to store data relating to **Subjects** with appropriate field names and data types using the sample data shown in Table 11.6.

Table 11.6

Subject Code	ICW520
Subject Title	Database Methods
Core Module	0
Vocational Module	1
Elective Module	0

Set the Subject Code field as the primary key. Save the table as **Subjects**. Do not enter data in the table at this point.

Task 10   Create a form linked to the Subjects table. Add all fields to the form. A suggested layout and format for the form is shown in Figure 11.5.
Save the form as **Subject Details**.

Task 11   Using the subject details form, enter all the records displayed in Table 11.7.

Note: Entering 1 or 0 in the Core, Vocational and Elective Module fields is equivalent to entering yes or no. By entering 1 or 0 instead of yes or no, it will be easier to determine which students are eligible for a full certificate later on in the assignment. To be eligible for a full certificate a student must have a pass, merit or distinction in 2 core modules, 5 or more vocational modules and 1 elective module.

Subject Details

IT College
Windy Ridge
Cork

Subject Code [ ]

Subject Title [ ]

Core Module [ ]
Vocational Module [ ]
Elective Module [ ]

Figure 11.5

Table 11.7

Subject Code	Subject Title	Core Module	Vocational Module	Elective Module
C301	Programming	0	1	0
C302	Software Development	0	1	0
C303	Systems Analysis	0	1	0
I201	Computer Maintenance	0	1	0
I202	Information and Communication Systems	0	1	0
IC621	Spreadsheet Methods	0	1	0
ICW400	Communications	1	0	0
ICW401	Work Experience	1	0	0
ICW402	Customer Service	0	0	1
ICW520	Database Methods	0	1	0
IW701	Word Processing	0	1	0
W101	Web Authoring	0	1	0
W102	Graphic Design	0	1	0
W103	E-Commerce	0	1	0

Task 12 Create a table to store data relating to **exams** with appropriate field names and data types using the sample data shown in Table 11.8.

Table 11.8

Exam Number	1
Student Code	03IT001
Subject Code	ICW520
Exam Period	Summer 2003
Exam Date	02/05/2003
Result	Merit

- Set the data type of the Exam Number field to autonumber.
- Set the Exam Number field as the primary key.
- Ensure that the data type and field sizes for Student Code and Subject Code are the same as those specified in the Students and Subjects tables. This is important so that we can link the tables.

Save the table as **Exams**. Do not enter data in the table at this point.

 Task 13   Add the exams table and subjects table to the relationship structure.

┌───── Relationships button	┌───── Show Table button

Figure 11.6   **Figure 11.7**

- Click the Relationships button and then click the Show Table button.
- Add the Exams table and Subjects table to the relationships window.

The relationship between the **Students** table and the **Exams** table is one-to-many. Each student can do many exams. The linking field is Student Code. Each student has a unique student code and that code only occurs once in the Students table. Each Student Code can occur many times in the Exams table. For example, if student 03IT001 does five exams, then the Student Code 03IT001 will appear five times in the Exams table.

To set up the relationship between Students and Exams, drag Student Code from the Students table and drop on Student Code in the Exams table. Click the Enforce Referential Integrity box and then click Create.

The relationship between the **Subjects** table and the **Exams** table is also one-to-many. Each subject can be examined many times. The linking field is Subject Code. Each subject has a unique Subject Code and that code only occurs once in the Subjects table. Each Subject Code can occur many times in the Exams table. For example, if there were ten database methods (ICW520) exams, the code ICW520 will appear ten times in the exams Table.

To set up the relationship between Subjects and Exams, drag Subject Code from the Subjects table and drop on Subject Code in the Exams table. Click the Enforce Referential Integrity box and then click Create.

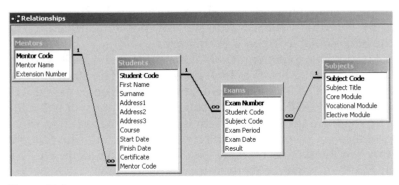

Figure 11.8

The tables should now appear in the relationships window, as shown in Figure 11.8.

Summary of relationships

It is very useful to have an overall view of the relationships in a database because data entry always starts on the 'one' side of the relationship: i.e. students data entry can't be completed unless data relating to mentors has already been entered. Exams data entry can't be completed unless data relating to students and subjects has already been entered.

Table 11.9

Tables	Relationship Type
Mentors and Students	One-To-Many
Students and Exams	One-To-Many
Subjects and Exams	One-To-Many
Students and Subjects	Many-To-Many

The relationship between the Students table and the subjects table is called a many-to-many relationship. Each student can do many exams. Each subject can be examined many times. In a many-to-many relationship the two tables (Students and subjects) are linked through a third table, in this case the Exams table, which contains fields linking it to both the Students table and the Subjects table.

The Exam Registration form

Each time a student is registered for an exam, data is entered in the Exam Number, Student Code, Subject Code and Exam Period fields in the Exams table. By entering a student code we are specifying which of the students stored in the Students table is sitting the exam. By entering a subject code we are specifying which of the subjects stored in the Subjects table is being examined.

It would be almost impossible to remember all of the student and subject codes. For this reason we will use combo boxes to look up the codes. The Student Code combo box will display student codes and student names but will enter the student codes. The Subject combo box will display the subject names but will enter the subject codes. Because there are two students with the same name, it is important that Student Code combo box displays both the Student Code and the Student Name. To ensure that we know which code relates to which student, we will include the Firstname and Surname fields from the Students table.

Because the Exam Registration form is based on two tables (Exams and Students) the fields required from each table must firstly be added to a query.

 Task 14 Create a new query and add the Students table and the Exams table.

From the Students table add the Firstname and Surname field.

From the Exams table add the Exam Number, Student Code, Subject Code and Exam Period fields.

Save the query as **Join tables for exam registration**.

 Task 15 Create a form linked to Join tables for exam registration. Add all fields to the form. The form title is Exam Registration.

• **Create a combo box for the Student Code field.**
Select 'I want the combo box to look up values in a table or query' and then select the Students table.
Add Student Code, Firstname and Surname to the combo box.
Because there are two John Murphy's, the key column must be displayed. Remove the tick from the hide key column box.
Select Student Code as the value in the combo box to store in the database and store this value in the Student Code field.
Enter 'Student' as the label for the combo box.
• **Create a combo box for the Subject Code field.**
Select 'I want the combo box to look up values in a table or query' and then select the Subjects table.
Add Subject Code and Subject Title to the combo box.
This time, hide the key column. (*There aren't any subjects with the same name.*)
Store the value in the Subject Code field.
Enter 'Subject' as the label for the combo box.
View the properties of the combo box. Set the column widths to 0 cm;10 cm and the list width to 10 cm. This makes the list wide enough to display 'information and communication systems'.

 Note: Selecting the hide key column box in the combo box wizard sets the width of column 1 of the combo box to 0 cm.

- **Create a combo box for the Exam Period field.**
  This time select 'I will type in the values'. The values to be displayed in the combo box are shown in Table 11.10.

Table 11.10

Exam Period (Combo Box)
Summer 2003
Christmas 2003
Summer 2004
Christmas 2004
Summer 2005
Christmas 2005

Set the limit to list property of the combo box to Yes. Set the tab stop property to No for the Exam Number, Firstname and Surname fields. (*Because Exam Number is an autonumber, you will not enter data in this field.*) Ensure that the top three fields in the tab order are Student Code, Subject Code and Exam Period.
A suggested layout and format for the form is shown in Figure 11.9.

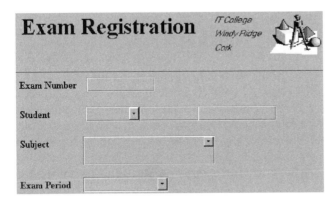

Figure 11.9

Save the form as **Exam Registration**.

 Task 16   Using the Exam Registration form, register the following students for **Database Methods, Communications, Word Processing and Information and Communication Systems** for the summer 2003 exam period.

 Note: If your exam numbers don't start at 1, it doesn't really matter. What is important is that every record should have a unique exam number.

Maura Clohosey
Tony Gallagher
Michael O Neill
John Murphy (03IT004)
Deirdre Moroney
Colin Evans
Eamonn Twomey
Nora Sheehan
Susan Wright
Sean Noonan

Register the following students for **Database Methods, Communications, Programming and Software Development** for the summer 2003 exam period.

Domnic Brennan
Brendan Dunne
Tadhg Scanlan
Diarmuid Scott
Rod Hogan

Register the following students for **Database Methods, Communications, Word Processing and E-Commerce** for the summer 2003 exam period.

Ciara Mooney
Robin Carr
Elaine Mc Carthy
Paula King
John Murphy (03WD005)

Although the registration of students for exams generates a lot of records, the autoNumber field and the combo boxes in the Exam Registration form make the task of data entry much easier. Once you have inputted all the data, you should have 80 records in the Exams table. Check this by opening the Exams table in datasheet view. 'record 1 of 80' should appear on the bottom left of the screen.

 Task 17   Create a query to find exam registrations by subject and period.

• Create a new query and add the Students, Exams and Subjects tables, in that order. (*Adding the Tables in a different order makes it difficult to understand the relationships between the Tables.*)
• From the Students table, add the Student Code, Firstname, Surname and Course fields. From the Exams table, add the Exam Number, Exam Period, Exam Date and Result fields. From the Subjects table, add the Subject Title field.
• Set up the query so that it displays the message 'Enter exam period' and then displays the message 'Enter subject title' when it is run. The query should then find all exam registrations relating to the exam period and subject title entered by the user **for which no exam date and no result has been entered**.

- Test the query by running it and entering summer 2003 as the exam period and programming as the subject title. It should find 5 records. Save the query as **Find student registrations by subject**.

Task 18 Create a new report linked to Find student registrations by subject.

- Add the Subject Title, Exam Period, Firstname, Surname and Course fields.
- Sort the report in ascending order of Student Code.
- Select Corporate as the report style.
- The report title is **Exam Lists by Subject**.
- In report design, move the Subject Title and Exam Period fields from the detail section to the report header.
- Include the college address and logo in the report header.
- Draw a label box in the report header and enter text relating to students who are not registered for the exam, as shown in Figure 11.10. This is an extract from the report. Test the report by previewing it a number of times and entering a different subject each time.

```
                                    IT College
                                    Windy Ridge
                                    Cork
Communications

Summer 2003 Exam List

If you would like to sit this exam but your name is
not listed below, please contact your mentor as soon
as possible

Student Name                    Course

Domnic          Brennan         Computer Programming

Brendan         Dunne           Computer Programming

Tadhg           Scanlan         Computer Programming

Diamuid         Scott           Computer Programming
```

Figure 11.10

 Tip: Copy the college address and logo from one of the forms and paste it into the report header.

Combining text, functions and fields in a text box

Consider the following statement: 'There are 20 students sitting the Communications exam'. Up to now, we have used a combination of labels, text boxes and fields to produce a statement like this. Three labels, a function and a field would be required to make up this statement. The labels, function and field would need to be positioned in such a way that in report preview they appear as a continuous sentence, as shown in Table 11.11.

If we previewed the report and entered summer 2003 as the exam period and communications as the subject title, the statement would be 'There are 20 students sitting the communications exam'.

Table 11.11

Label	Text Box	Label	Field	Label
There are	=count([Surname])	students sitting the	[Subject Title]	Exam

Instead of using separate labels, text boxes and fields, this statement can be produced by entering one report formula in a text box. Text must be enclosed in inverted commas. Labels, text boxes and fields are 'joined' using the '&' symbol.

Task 19   Create a text box in the report footer of the Exam Lists by Subject report. Enter the following report formula in the text box:
  = "there are" & count([surname]) & "students sitting the" & [subject title]& "exam"

Delete the label attached to the text box. Preview the report and enter Summer 2003 as the Exam Period and Programming as the Subject Title. 'There are 5 students sitting the Programming exam' should appear at the bottom of the report.

Tip: Include a space at the end of each text string. Include a space at the beginning of the second and third text strings.

Task 20   Print the Exam Lists by Subject report for each exam.

Task 21   Create a report that produces disk labels by subject. When the report is previewed the message 'Enter exam period' followed by the message 'Enter subject title' should appear. The report should produce disk labels for the subject entered by the user. Save this report as **Disk Labels by Subject**. A sample label is shown below.

Table 11.12

Summer 2003
03IT001
Maura Clohosey
Database Methods
Exam Number: 11

Tip: This report can also be linked to Find Student Registrations by Subject.

Entering exam results

To enter exam results efficiently, we need to specify a number of conditions:

1. Only exams relating to the subject and exam period we specify should be displayed.
2. Only records where the result field is empty should be displayed.

These conditions can be entered in a query. A form to enter exam results will be linked to the query.

 Task 22 Create a new query and add the Students, Exams and Subjects tables.

- From the Students table add Student Code, Firstname and Surname. From the Exams table, add Exam Period, Exam Date and Result. From the Subjects table add Subject Title.
- Add parameters to the query so that when it is run, we are asked to enter an exam period and a subject title.
- Enter a condition so that only records where the Result field is empty are displayed.
- Sort the query in ascending order on the Student Code field. Save the query as **Exams with no results entered**.

 Task 23 Create a form linked to the Exams with no results entered query.

- Add all fields to the form. The form title is **Enter Exam Results**.
- Move the Exam Period field from the detail section to the form header.
- Set the enabled property to no for the Student Code, Firstname, Surname, Subject Title and Exam Period fields.
- Create a combo box for the Results field. Select 'I will type in the values' which are Distinction, Merit, Pass, Fail. A suggested layout and format for the form is shown in Figure 11.11.

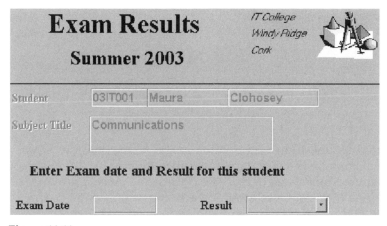

Figure 11.11

 Macros

A macro is a list of commands, specified by the user, which are executed in quick succession by Access when the macro is run. Macros can be linked to events. For example, the event of clicking a button can trigger a macro into action. Macros can be created to carry out common database tasks, such as finding and adding records. Macros can also be used to develop a user interface by creating custom menus, making it easier and quicker for the database user to carry out tasks. Our first macro relates to the Enter Exam Results form. Because the Enter Exam Results form is linked to the exams with no results entered query, we will be asked to enter an exam period and a subject title each time we open the form. This speeds up data entry. Because the form displays a very specific set of records, the number of records to scroll through is minimised once we enter a specific exam period and subject title. One downside of linking the form to a parameter query is that we would have to close the form and open it again, entering a different subject title, in order to enter results for another subject.

In the following example, we will create a macro, which has two commands. The first command will close the Enter Exam Results form and the second command will open it again. The macro will be linked to a command button, which will be placed on the Enter Exam Results form. If database users want to enter results for a second subject, they simply click the button. Once they click the button, the form will close and immediately open again and they will be asked to enter an exam period and subject title so that the next set of results can be entered. This is much quicker and easier than manually closing the Enter Exam Results form and then opening it again.

 Creating a macro

1. In the database window, select Macros and then click New. A new macro window is displayed, as shown in Figure 11.12.

Macro1 : Macro	
Action	Comment
▼	

Figure 11.12

A macro is created by specifying commands in the action column. When the macro is run, the commands will be executed in sequence by the macro. The good news is that you don't have to type the commands. Access provides a list of macro commands that can be selected in each line of the action column. All you have to do is figure out which commands you need and then put them in the correct sequence.

It is good programming practice to enter comments in your macro. A comment is usually a short statement describing the function of a particular line in the macro. If you don't enter comments, you may find it difficult to remember the purpose of the macro the next time you edit it. Comments have no effect on the operation of the macro.

2. Select the Close command in the first line of the action column.

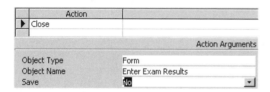

Figure 11.13

In Action Arguments select Form as the object type, Enter Exam Results as the object name and save=No, as shown in Figure 11.13.

Note: Save=No relates to saving changes to the design of the form. When save is set to no, any design changes the database user makes to the form will not be saved when the form is closed by the macro. It does not affect the entering of records in the form.

3. Select the OpenForm command in the second line of the action column. In action arguments, select Enter Exam Results as the object name.
4. Click the save button and type **Next set of results** as the macro name.

Running a macro from a command button

1. Open the Enter Exam Results form in design view.
2. Click the Toolbox button if the toolbox is not already displayed.

Figure 11.14

3. Check that the control wizard is on and then click the Command Button.
4. Click and drag to draw a rectangle in the detail section to the right of the Surname text box.
5. The command button wizard asks you 'What action do you want to happen when the button is pressed?' Select Miscellaneous from the categories box and then select Run Macro from the actions box. Click Next.
6. Select **Next set of results** as the macro that the command button will run. Click Next.
7. A picture or text can be inserted in the command button. Select the text option. Delete run macro and type Next Subject. Click Next.
8. Type **exam results button** as the button name and click Finish.
9. View the properties of the button and set the tab stop to No.
10. Change the font colour of the button text (Next Subject) to navy and the font weight to bold.
11. Save the Enter Exam Results form and then click the Form View button. Enter Summer 2003 as the Exam Period and Communications as the Subject Title. The form displays 20 records.

12. Click the Next Subject button. Enter Summer 2003 as the exam period and Programming as the subject title. The form displays 5 records.

Editing a macro

To ensure that the Enter Exam Results form is maximised when it is opened, we will add another line to the Next set of results Macro.

1. In the database window, click Macros, select the **Next set of results** macro and then click Design.
2. In the next line below the OpenForm command, select Maximize in the action column. (*This ensures that the Enter Exam Results form occupies all of the available window when it is opened.*)
3. Click the Save button to save the macro and then close the macro.

Creating a command button to close the enter exam results form

Access has a command button wizard that can be used to automate simple operations such as opening and closing forms and reports as well as record navigation. If the operation you wish to automate is included in the command button wizard, there is no need to create a macro. Once you draw a command button, the wizard brings you through a series of steps, asking you what should happen when the button is clicked and writes code in the background to implement this.

1. In design view of the Enter Exam Results form, click the command button and draw a button immediately below the Next Subject button.
2. In the categories box, select Form Operations. In the actions box, select Close Form. Click Next.
3. Select the text option and replace Close Form with **Exit**. Click Next.
4. Type **close exam results button** as the button name and click Finish.
5. View the properties of the button and set the tab stop to No.
6. Using the format painter, copy the format from the Next Subject button to the Exit button.
7. Set the width of both buttons to 2.275 cm (0.91 inches) and the height of both buttons to 0.714 cm (0.286 inches).
8. Click the Save button to save the changes to the design of the Enter Exam Results form.

Task 24 Using the Enter Exam Results form enter the exam results displayed in Table 11.13.

Tip: To speed up entering the date in the Exam Date field, enter 02/05/ 2003 in the Exam Date field for Domnic Brennan. Now highlight 02/05/ 2003 and click the copy button. The date can now be pasted into the Exam Date text box each time you are entering an exam result either by clicking the paste button or by holding down the CTRL key and typing v.

Table 11.13

Exam Period   Summer 2003
Subject Title   Database Methods
Date of Exam   02/05/2003

Student Number	Student Name	Result
03CP001	Domnic Brennan	Merit
03CP002	Brendan Dunne	Pass
03CP003	Tadhg Scanlan	Distinction
03CP004	Diarmuid Scott	Fail
03CP005	Rod Hogan	Merit
03IT001	Maura Clohosey	Merit
03IT002	Tony Gallagher	Merit
03IT003	Michael O Neill	Merit
03IT004	John Murphy	Fail
03IT005	Deirdre Moroney	Merit
03IT006	Colin Evans	Distinction
03IT007	Eamonn Twomey	Distinction
03IT008	Nora Sheehan	Pass
03IT009	Susan Wright	Merit
03IT010	Sean Noonan	Merit
03WD001	Ciara Mooney	Distinction
03WD002	Robin Carr	Distinction
03WD003	Elaine Mc Carthy	Distinction
03WD004	Paula King	Pass
03WD005	John Murphy	Distinction

Click the Next Subject button and enter Communications results displayed in Table 11.14.

Table 11.14

Exam Period		Summer 2003
Subject Title		Communications
Date of Exam		05/05/2003

Student Number	Student Name	Result
03CP001	Domnic Brennan	Distinction
03CP002	Brendan Dunne	Merit
03CP003	Tadhg Scanlan	Distinction
03CP004	Diarmuid Scott	Pass
03CP005	Rod Hogan	Merit
03IT001	Maura Clohosey	Pass
03IT002	Tony Gallagher	Fail
03IT003	Michael O Neill	Merit
03IT004	John Murphy	Pass
03IT005	Deirdre Moroney	Distinction
03IT006	Colin Evans	Merit
03IT007	Eamonn Twomey	Merit
03IT008	Nora Sheehan	Merit
03IT009	Susan Wright	Fail
03IT010	Sean Noonan	Pass
03WD001	Ciara Mooney	Merit
03WD002	Robin Carr	Distinction
03WD003	Elaine Mc Carthy	Distinction
03WD004	Paula King	Merit
03WD005	John Murphy	Merit

Click the Next Subject button and enter Word Processing results displayed in Table 11.15 on page 199.

Table 11.15

Exam Period	Summer 2003
Subject Title	Word Processing
Date of Exam	07/05/2003

Student Number	Student Name	Result
03IT001	Maura Clohosey	Distinction
03IT002	Tony Gallagher	Merit
03IT003	Michael O Neill	Distinction
03IT004	John Murphy	Merit
03IT005	Deirdre Moroney	Distinction
03IT006	Colin Evans	Distinction
03IT007	Eamonn Twomey	Distinction
03IT008	Nora Sheehan	Merit
03IT009	Susan Wright	Merit
03IT010	Sean Noonan	Pass
03WD001	Ciara Mooney	Distinction
03WD002	Robin Carr	Merit
03WD003	Elaine Mc Carthy	Merit
03WD004	Paula King	Fail
03WD005	John Murphy	Distinction

Click the next subject button and enter information and communication systems results displayed in Table 11.16 on page 200. Deirdre Moroney did not sit the information and communication systems exam.

Click the next subject button and enter Programming results displayed in the Table 11.17 on page 200.

Click the next subject button and enter Software Development results displayed in the Table 11.18 on page 201.

Click the next subject button and enter E-Commerce results displayed in Table 11.19.

Paula King did not sit the E-Commerce exam.

Click the Exit button to close the Enter Exam Results form.

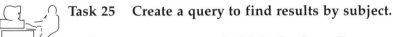

Task 25   Create a query to find results by subject.

- Create a new query and add the Students, Exams and Subjects tables. From the Students table add Firstname, Surname and Course. From the Exams table, add Exam Period, Exam Date and Result. From the Subjects table add Subject Title.
- Add parameters to the query so that when it is run, we are asked to enter an exam period and a subject title.

Table 11.16

Exam Period	Summer 2003
Subject Title	Information and Communication Systems
Date of Exam	09/05/2003

Student Number	Student Name	Result
03IT001	Maura Clohosey	Merit
03IT002	Tony Gallagher	Pass
03IT003	Michael O Neill	Distinction
03IT004	John Murphy	Fail
03IT006	Colin Evans	Distinction
03IT007	Eamonn Twomey	Merit
03IT008	Nora Sheehan	Pass
03IT009	Susan Wright	Pass
03IT010	Sean Noonan	Fail

Table 11.17

Exam Period	Summer 2003
Subject Title	Programming
Date of Exam	12/05/2003

Student Number	Student Name	Result
03CP001	Domnic Brennan	Distinction
03CP002	Brendan Dunne	Pass
03CP003	Tadhg Scanlan	Merit
03CP004	Diarmuid Scott	Pass
03CP005	Rod Hogan	Distinction

- Enter conditions so that only records where the Exam Date and Result fields contain data are displayed.
- Save the query as **Find results by subject**.

Task 26 Create a report to display results by subject.

- Create a new report linked to the Find results by subject query. Add all fields except for Exam Date to the report.

Table 11.18

Exam Period	Summer 2003
Subject Title	Software Development
Date of Exam	14/05/2003

Student Number	Student Name	Result
03CP001	Domnic Brennan	Merit
03CP002	Brendan Dunne	Merit
03CP003	Tadhg Scanlan	Distinction
03CP004	Diarmuid Scott	Fail
03CP005	Rod Hogan	Pass

Table 11.19

Exam Period	Summer 2003
Subject Title	E-Commerce
Date of Exam	15/05/2003

Student Number	Student Name	Result
03WD001	Ciara Mooney	Merit
03WD002	Robin Carr	Distinction
03WD003	Elaine Mc Carthy	Merit
03WD005	John Murphy	Distinction

- Group the report by Result. Sort the report in ascending order of Surname.
- Select Corporate as the report style.
- The report title is **Results by Subject**.
- Delete the label containing 'Results by Subject' in the report header. Create a text box in its place and enter a formula which creates a different report title depending on which subject is entered in the parameter value dialog box as follows: Communications Results, Database Results and so on.

Hint: Use & to join a field name and text in the text box.
- Move the Exam Period field from the detail section to the report header below the main heading. Delete the Subject Title field from the detail section.
- Delete all labels and lines from the page header.
- Add a function to the report to calculate the total number of distinctions, merits, passes and fails. A suggested layout and format for the report is displayed in Figure 11.15 on page 202, an extract from the report, where communications was entered as the Subject Title.

Preview the report for each of the remaining subjects in which there were exams. Print each report. The one-to-many relationship between Subjects and Exams can be seen clearly in these reports. Each subject can generate many exams.

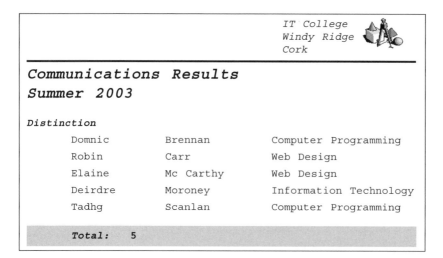

IT College
Windy Ridge
Cork

Communications Results
Summer 2003

Distinction

Domnic	Brennan	Computer Programming
Robin	Carr	Web Design
Elaine	Mc Carthy	Web Design
Deirdre	Moroney	Information Technology
Tadhg	Scanlan	Computer Programming

Total: 5

Figure 11.15

Task 27 Create a report to display the number of distinctions, merits, passes and fails in all subjects.

- Create a new query and add the Exams and Subjects tables. From the Exams table, add Exam Period and Result. From the Subjects table add Subject Title.
- Add a parameter to the query so that when it is run, we are asked to enter an exam period.
- Enter a condition so that only records where the Result field contains data are displayed.
- Save the query as **Find results for a specific period**.
- Create a new report linked to the Find results for a specific period query. Add all fields to the report.
- Group the report firstly by the Subject Title field and then by the Result field.
- Select Corporate as the report style.
- The report title is **Exam Results Analysis**.
- Move the Exam Period field from the detail section to the report header below the main heading.
- Add a count function to the result header to count the number of results per grade.
- Reduce the height of the detail section to 0 cm (0 inches).
- Add a count function to the Subject Title footer to count the number of results per subject. (**Hint:** *Refer to the Subject Title field.*)

A suggested layout and format for the report is displayed in an extract from the report in Figure 11.16 on page 203, where Summer 2003 was entered as the exam period:

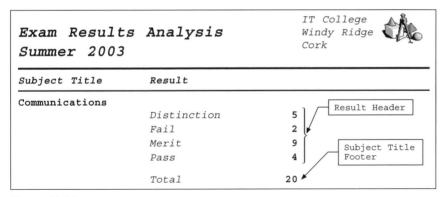

Figure 11.16

Task 28   Find exam results of current students.

- Create a new query and add the Students, Exams and Subjects tables. From the Students table add the Student Code, Firstname, Surname, Course and Finish Date fields. From the Exams table, add Result. From the Subjects table add Subject Title.
- Add conditions to the query so that it only finds records where data has been entered in the Result field and where data hasn't been entered in the Finish Date field.
- Save the query as **Results of current students**.

Task 29   Display student results.

- Create a new report linked to the Results of current students query.
- Add all fields, except for Finish Date, to the report.
- Group the report firstly by Course and then by Student Code.
- Select Corporate as the report style.
- The report title is **Results by Student**.
- Adjust the group properties to keep groups together on the same page.
- Add a function to the report that displays today's date beneath the report title.
- Add a formula to the report to calculate the total number of exam results for each course. This formula should produce three statements in the report as follows: 'Number of exams taken by Computer Programming students: 20', 'Number of exams taken by Information Technology students: 39' and 'Number of exams taken by Web Design students: 19'. (*These totals will increase as more exam results are entered in the database*).

A suggested layout and format for the report is displayed in Figure 11.17 on page 204. This report was previewed on 22 May 2003.

The one-to-many relationship between Students and Exams can be seen clearly in this report. Each student can do many exams.

Task 30   Create a student report.

- Create a new query and add the Students, Exams and Subjects tables. From the Students table add the Student Code, Firstname, Surname,

```
                                                    IT College
                                                    Windy Ridge
                                                    Cork

        ──────────────────────────────────────────────────────────

        Results by Student
        22/05/2003

        Computer Programming

        03CP001   Domnic     Brennan
                                    Communications              Distinction
                                    Database Methods            Merit
                                    Programming                 Distinction
                                    Software Development        Merit

        03CP002   Brendan    Dunne
                                    Communications              Merit
                                    Database Methods            Pass
                                    Programming                 Pass
                                    Software Development        Merit
```

Figure 11.17

Course, Finish Date and Certificate fields. From the Exams table, add Result. From the Subjects table add Subject Title, Core Module, Vocational Module and Elective Module.
- Add conditions to the query so that it finds records of exams where the result was pass, merit or distinction and where data hasn't been entered in the Finish Date field and where Certificate is equal to No.
- Save the query as **Certification Query**.
- Create a report linked to Certification Query including all fields except for Core Module, Vocational Module, Elective Module, Certificate and Finish Date.
- Group the report by Student Code.
- Select Corporate as the report style.
- The report title is **Student Certificates**.
- Move the Firstname, Surname and Course fields from the detail section to the Student Code Header.
- In the Student Code Header delete the Student Code field.
- Add a function to the Student Code Header that displays today's date.
- Delete labels and lines contained in the report header.
- Reduce the height of the report header to 0 cm (0 inches).
- View the properties of the Student Code Header. Set the Force New Page property to Before Section. This means that details relating to each student will be on a separate page.

 Tip: To eliminate large gaps between the firstname and surname fields, create a text box in the Student Code Header and type the following formula:

=[Firstname] & " " & [Surname]

A suggested layout and format for the report is displayed as follows. This report was previewed on 22 May 2003.

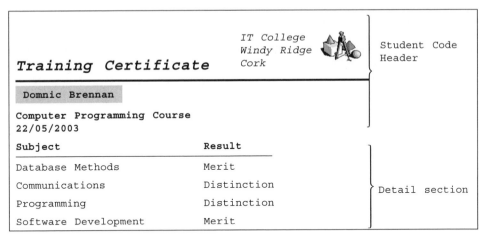

Figure 11.18

Scroll through the report. It should contain 20 pages with a separate training certificate on each page.

Task 31 Create a report summary for each student.
Create a report summary, as shown in Figure 11.9, in the Student Code Footer. (*Totals displayed are for Domnic Brennan.*)

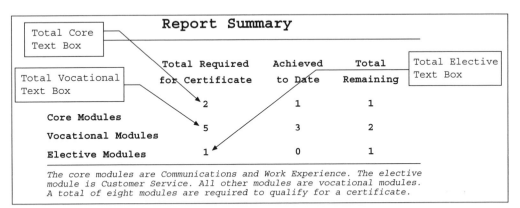

Figure 11.19

Important points:

1. **Total required for certificate:**   The number of core, vocational and elective modules required to qualify for a certificate are fixed numbers. They are not stored anywhere in the database. To display these numbers, create three text boxes positioned, as shown in Figure 11.19. In the top text box enter the formula =2. View the properties of this text box and enter Total Core as the name. In the middle text box, enter the formula =5. View the properties of this text box and

enter Total Vocational as the Name. Enter =1 in the bottom text box. View the properties of this text box and Enter Total Elective as the name.

2. **Achieved to date:** The total number of core, vocational and elective modules achieved to date is calculated using the sum function in three separate text boxes.

3. **Total remaining:** To calculate the total number of core, vocational and elective modules to be completed, subtract the number of modules achieved to date from the total number of modules required. Example: =[Total Core]–sum([Core Module]) calculates the number of core modules remaining. Similar formulas are required for vocational and elective modules.

4. The explanation at the bottom of the report summary is entered in a label box.

A sample page of the completed report is displayed in Figure 11.20. This report was previewed on 22 May 2003.

Training Certificate   IT College
                                          Windy Ridge
                                          Cork

Domnic Brennan

Computer Programming Course

22/05/2003

Subject	Result
Database Methods	Merit
Communications	Distinction
Programming	Distinction
Software Development	Merit

Report Summary

	Total Required for Certificate	Achieved to Date	Total Remaining
Core Modules	2	1	1
Vocational Modules	5	3	2
Elective Modules	1	0	1

The core modules are Communications and Work experience. The elective module is Customer Service. All other modules are vocational modules. A total of eight modules are required to qualify for a certificate.

Figure 11.20

Task 32 Create a letter to accompany student reports.

- Create a new query and add the Mentors and Students tables. From the Mentors table add the Mentor Name field. From the Students table add the Firstname, Surname, Address1, Address2, Address3, Course and Finish Date fields.

- Add a condition to the query so that it only finds students who don't have a finish date. Save the query as **Students receiving certificates**.
- Create the letter displayed below using Microsoft Word. **(Don't type the field names, displayed in bold print.)**

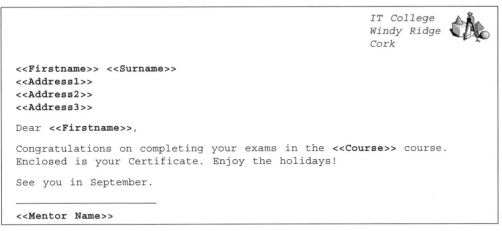

```
                                                      IT College
                                                      Windy Ridge
                                                      Cork

<<Firstname>>  <<Surname>>
<<Address1>>
<<Address2>>
<<Address3>>

Dear <<Firstname>>,

Congratulations on completing your exams in the <<Course>> course.
Enclosed is your Certificate. Enjoy the holidays!

See you in September.

_____

<<Mentor Name>>
```

Figure 11.21

- Save the letter as **certificate notice**.
- Using the Mail Merge facility set this letter up as a main document. Use the **Students receiving certificates** query as the data source and insert fields from the database, shown in bold print above.
- Merge the main document with the data source to produce a new document containing 20 letters. Save this document as **Certificate Notifications Summer 2003**.

Task 33   In Microsoft Access, use the label wizard to produce labels for all students receiving letters. Each label should have the Firstname, Surname, Address1, Address2 and Address3 fields and should be set up as in Table 11.20.

Table 11.20

Domnic Brennan
The Heath
Fermoy
Co. Cork

Sort the labels in ascending order of surname. The report name is **labels for certificate letters.**

Creating a custom menu system

To streamline use of the Exam Management System database and to make it more user-friendly, we will create a menu system using a series of forms containing command buttons. By clicking the command buttons, the database user will be able to access forms and reports stored in the database. When the menu system is completed, the database window will no longer be visible to the database user. The functions of the Exam Management System database can be divided into two broad categories:

1. Data entry
2. Reporting

To allow easy access to data entry and reporting, we will create three custom menus as follows:

1. Main menu
2. Data Entry menu
3. Reports menu

Creating the data entry menu

1. Create a new form in design view. Do not link the form to a table or query.
2. Increase the size of the detail section until it occupies the entire screen.
3. Draw a label box at the top left of the form. Enter the text DATA ENTRY MENU in the label box. Format this text to Arial, 26, bold.
4. Copy the college address and logo from any of the other forms and position to the right of the heading.
5. Save the form as **Data Entry Menu**.

Creating command buttons to open forms

1. In design view of Data Entry Menu, check that the control wizard is on and then draw a command button below the title.
2. Select Form Operations in the categories box and Open Form in the actions box. Click Next.
3. Select Student Registration as the form to open. Click Next.
4. Select open the form and show all the records. Click Next.
5. Select MS Access form as the button picture. Click Next.
6. Enter **student reg button** as the button name. Click Finish.
7. Draw a label box to the right of the button and enter the text **Register new students.**
8. Format the label text to Arial, bold, italic, font size 12.
9. Click the save button to save the Data Entry Menu form.

Task 34 Following the steps described above, create command buttons to open the Exam Registration and Enter Exam Results forms.

Displayed in Figure 11.22 is a suggested layout and format for the Data Entry Menu form.

DATA ENTRY MENU

IT College
Windy Ridge
Cork

🖹   *Register new students*

🖹   *Register students for exams*

🖹   *Enter exam results*

📲   *Exit*

Figure 11.22

NOTE

Note: The Exit button can be created by selecting Form Operations in the categories box and Close Form in the actions box.

Creating the reports menu

1. Rather than creating a new form, select the Data Entry Menu form in the database window. Click the copy button on the toolbar and then click paste.
2. Enter **Reports Menu** as the name for the new form.
3. In design view of the Reports Menu form change the title to REPORTS MENU.
4. Delete all command buttons and labels except for the exit command button and label.

Creating command buttons to preview reports

1. In design view of the Reports Menu form draw a command button below the title.
2. Select Report Operations from categories and Preview Report from actions. Click Next.
3. Select Exam Lists by Subject from the list of reports. Click Next.
4. Select MS Access Report 1 as the button picture. Click Next.
5. Enter **exam reg button** as the button name. Click Finish.
6. Draw a label box to the right of the button and enter the text Exam Registrations by Subject.
7. Format the label text to Arial, bold, italic, font size 12.
8. Click the save button to save the Reports Menu form.

Task 35 Following the step described above, create command buttons to preview the reports listed in Table 11.21. Create a label to the right of each button and enter label text as specified.

Table 11.21

Create command buttons to preview each of the reports listed below	Label Text to the right of the command button
Disk Labels by Subject	Print Exam Disk Labels
Results by Student	View Exam Results by Student
Results by Subject	View Exam Results by Subject
Exam Results Analysis	Analyse Results by Exam Period
List of Current Students	View current list of Students by Course
Mentor Groups	View current Students by Mentor Group
Student Certificates	View Certificates for Current Students
Labels for certificate letters	Print Mailing Labels for Certificates

Displayed in Figure 11.23 is a suggested layout and format for the Reports Menu form.

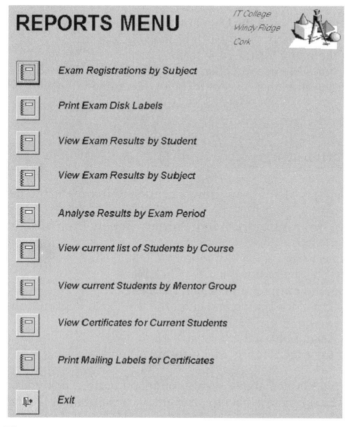

Figure 11.23

Creating the main menu

We will create the Main Menu form by copying an existing form.

1. In the database window select the Data Entry Menu form. Click the copy button on the toolbar and then click paste.
2. Enter **Main Menu** as the name for the new form.
3. In design view of the Main Menu form change the title to IT COLLEGE EXAM SYSTEM.
4. Delete all command buttons and labels.
5. Create a command button to open the Data Entry Menu form and a command button to open the Reports Menu form.

Displayed in Figure 11.24 is a suggested layout and format for the Main Menu form.

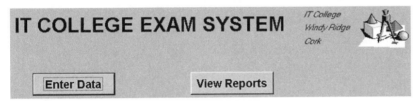

Figure 11.24

Autoexec macros

An autoexec macro is a macro that runs automatically each time you open a database. In the following example, we will create an autoexec macro that opens and maximises the Main Menu form. Once the macro has been created and saved with the name autoexec, the Exam Management System database will always open with the Main Menu form displayed. The database window will no longer be seen by the database user.

Creating an autoexec macro

1. In the database window, select Macros and then click New.
2. Select the OpenForm command in the first line of the action column. Select Main Menu as the form name.
3. Select the Maximize command in the second line of the action column.
4. Save the macro as **autoexec.**
5. To test the autoexec macro close the Exam Management System database and then open it again. The database should open with the Main Menu form displayed.

Task 36 In the main menu, click the Enter Data button and then click the Register students for exams button. Click the New Record button in the toolbar and register the following students for **Computer**

Maintenance, Spreadsheet Methods, Work Experience and Customer Service for the Christmas 2003 exam period.

Maura Clohosey
Tony Gallagher
Michael O Neill
John Murphy (03IT004)
Deirdre Moroney
Colin Evans
Eamonn Twomey
Nora Sheehan
Susan Wright
Sean Noonan

Register the following students for **Systems Analysis, Spreadsheet Methods, Work Experience and Customer Service** for the Christmas 2003 exam period.

Domnic Brennan
Brendan Dunne
Tadhg Scanlan
Diarmuid Scott
Rod Hogan

Register the following students for **Web Authoring, Graphic Design, Work Experience and Customer Service** for the Christmas 2003 exam period.

Ciara Mooney
Robin Carr
Elaine Mc Carthy
Paula King
John Murphy (03WD005)

 Task 37   Using the Print Exam Disk Labels button in the Reports Menu, preview and print disk labels for Spreadsheet Methods, Web Authoring and Graphic Design for the Christmas 2003 exam period.

Task 38   Using the Exam Registrations by Subject button in the Reports Menu, preview and print exam registrations for each subject in the Christmas 2003 exam period.

Task 39   In the Main Menu, click the Enter Data button and then click the Enter exam results button. Enter the exam results displayed in Table 11.22 on page 213.
   Click the Next Subject button and enter Spreadsheet Methods results displayed in Table 11.23 on page 213.

Table 11.22

Exam Period	Christmas 2003
Subject Title	Computer Maintenance
Date of Exam	09/12/2003

Student Number	Student Name	Result
03IT001	Maura Clohosey	Merit
03IT002	Tony Gallagher	Distinction
03IT003	Michael O Neill	Merit
03IT004	John Murphy	Pass
03IT005	Deirdre Moroney	Distinction
03IT006	Colin Evans	Distinction
03IT007	Eamonn Twomey	Merit
03IT008	Nora Sheehan	Pass
03IT009	Susan Wright	Pass
03IT010	Sean Noonan	Merit

Table 11.23

Exam Period	Christmas 2003
Subject Title	Spreadsheet Methods
Date of Exam	10/12/2003

Student Number	Student Name	Result
03CP001	Domnic Brennan	Distinction
03CP002	Brendan Dunne	Pass
03CP003	Tadhg Scanlan	Distinction
03CP004	Diarmuid Scott	Merit
03CP005	Rod Hogan	Merit
03IT001	Maura Clohosey	Merit
03IT002	Tony Gallagher	Merit
03IT003	Michael O Neill	Distinction
03IT004	John Murphy	Fail
03IT005	Deirdre Moroney	Distinction
03IT006	Colin Evans	Distinction
03IT007	Eamonn Twomey	Merit
03IT008	Nora Sheehan	Fail
03IT009	Susan Wright	Pass
03IT010	Sean Noonan	Pass

Click the Next Subject button and enter Work Experience results displayed in Table 11.24.

Table 11.24

Exam Period	Christmas 2003
Subject Title	Work Experience
Date of Exam	12/12/2003

Student Number	Student Name	Result
03CP001	Domnic Brennan	Merit
03CP002	Brendan Dunne	Fail
03CP003	Tadhg Scanlan	Merit
03CP004	Diarmuid Scott	Pass
03CP005	Rod Hogan	Merit
03IT001	Maura Clohosey	Distinction
03IT002	Tony Gallagher	Merit
03IT003	Michael O Neill	Distinction
03IT004	John Murphy	Pass
03IT005	Deirdre Moroney	Pass
03IT006	Colin Evans	Merit
03IT007	Eamonn Twomey	Distinction
03IT008	Nora Sheehan	Pass
03IT009	Susan Wright	Merit
03IT010	Sean Noonan	Merit
03WD001	Ciara Mooney	Distinction
03WD002	Robin Carr	Distinction
03WD003	Elaine Mc Carthy	Merit
03WD004	Paula King	Fail
03WD005	John Murphy	Merit

Click the Next Subject button and enter Customer Service results displayed in Table 11.25 (Tadhg Scanlan did not sit the Customer Service exam.)

Table 11.25

Exam Period	Christmas 2003
Subject Title	Customer Service
Date of Exam	15/12/2003

Student Number	Student Name	Result
03CP001	Domnic Brennan	Pass
03CP002	Brendan Dunne	Merit
03CP004	Diarmuid Scott	Merit
03CP005	Rod Hogan	Pass
03IT001	Maura Clohosey	Merit
03IT002	Tony Gallagher	Distinction
03IT003	Michael O Neill	Pass
03IT004	John Murphy	Distinction
03IT005	Deirdre Moroney	Merit
03IT006	Colin Evans	Fail
03IT007	Eamonn Twomey	Pass
03IT008	Nora Sheehan	Merit
03IT009	Susan Wright	Pass
03IT010	Sean Noonan	Pass
03WD001	Ciara Mooney	Distinction
03WD002	Robin Carr	Merit
03WD003	Elaine Mc Carthy	Distinction
03WD004	Paula King	Pass
03WD005	John Murphy	Merit

Click the Next Subject button and enter Systems Analysis results displayed in Table 11.26.

Table 11.26

Exam Period   Summer 2003
Subject Title   Systems Analysis
Date of Exam   16/12/2003

Student Number	Student Name	Result
03CP001	Domnic Brennan	Distinction
03CP002	Brendan Dunne	Merit
03CP003	Tadhg Scanlan	Merit
03CP004	Diarmuid Scott	Distinction
03CP005	Rod Hogan	Distinction

Click the Next Subject button and enter Web Authoring results displayed in Table 11.27.

Table 11.27

Exam Period   Christman 2003
Subject Title   Web Authoring
Date of Exam   16/12/2003

Student Number	Student Name	Result
03WD001	Ciara Mooney	Distinction
03WD002	Robin Carr	Distinction
03WD003	Elaine Mc Carthy	Distinction
03WD004	Paula King	Merit
03WD005	John Murphy	Distinction

Click the Next Subject button and enter Graphic Design results displayed in Table 11.28.

Table 11.28

Exam Period   Summer 2003
Subject Title   Graphic Design
Date of Exam   18/12/2003

Student Number	Student Name	Result
03WD001	Ciara Mooney	Merit
03WD002	Robin Carr	Merit
03WD003	Elaine Mc Carthy	Merit
03WD004	Paula King	Distinction
03WD005	John Murphy	Pass

Task 40 Edit the Student Certificates report so that each certificate fits on one page. Remove the page footer from the report.

Task 41 Using the Reports Menu, print all reports relating to exam results and certificates.

Finding students who qualify for a full certificate

To qualify for a full certificate, a student must have achieved a pass, merit or distinction in 2 core modules, 5 vocational modules and 1 elective module. We have already created a query named Certification Query that lists subjects passed by current students. This query displays a separate record for each exam passed by a student. For example, Paula King passed 5 exams so the certification query displays 5 records for Paula King. To determine which students qualify for a certificate, we must summarise data stored in the certification query so that only one record is displayed for each student with the total number of core, vocational and elective modules passed.

1. Create a new query **linked to Certification Query**. Add Student Code, Firstname, Surname, Course, Core Module, Vocational Module, Elective Module and Certificate to the query design grid.

Figure 11.25

2. Click the Totals button and select Sum in the totals row for the Core Module, Vocational Module and Elective Module fields.
3. Run the query. It should display 20 records with the total number of core, vocational and elective modules displayed for each student.
4. Click the design view button. Enter conditions in the query design grid so that the query finds students who have 2 core modules, 5 or more vocational modules and 1 elective module.
5. Run the query again. It should now display 9 records. Print the records found by the query.
6. Save this query as **Certification Query part 2**.
7. Create a new form linked to the Students table. Add the Student Code, Firstname, Surname and Certificate fields to the form. Save the form as **Award Certificate**. A suggested format and layout for the form is displayed in Figure 11.26.

Student Certification *IT College*
Windy Ridge
Cork

Student Code 03CP001

Name Domnic Brennan

Certificate ☐

Figure 11.26

8. Create a new command button that opens the Award Certificate form. Position the command button between the Enter exam results and Exit buttons on the Data Entry Menu form as displayed in Figure 11.27.

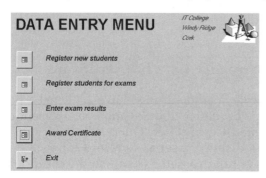

Figure 11.27

9. Using the Award Certificate form, tick the Certificate check box for each of the 9 students found by Certification Query part 2.

 Note: The Award Certificate form cannot be linked to Certification Query part 2 due to the fact that this query calculates totals. This problem can only be solved using techniques that are beyond the scope of this book.

Update queries

All of the queries we have created, up to this point, have been select queries. A Select Query simply finds and displays records. An Update Query, on the other hand, finds records and then updates these records by entering data in one or more fields or by altering existing data in one or more fields. We can create an update query to find all records of students who have received a full certificate and then enter today's date in the Finish Date field for each of these students.

1. Create a new query and add the Students table.
2. Add the Student Code, Firstname, Surname, Start Date, Certificate and Finish Date fields to the query.
3. Add a condition to the query so that it only finds records of students who have a certificate.
4. Test the query by running it. It should find 9 records.
5. In design view of the query, click the Query Type button shown in Figure 11.28 and select Update Query.
6. A new update-to-row appears in the query design grid.
7. Enter =date( ) in the update-to-row of the Finish Date field. When we run the query, today's date will be entered in the Finish Date field for all students who have a certificate.
8. Save the query as **Update finish date**.

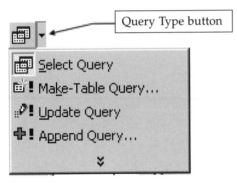

Query Type button

Select Query

Make-Table Query...

Update Query

Append Query...

Figure 11.28

9. Run the query. The message 'You are about to update 9 rows' is displayed. Click Yes to update the records.
10. Open the Students table in datasheet view. Check that there are 9 records with today's date entered in the Finish Date field.

This assignment has been an introduction to relational database. Many additional features could have been included in the Exam Management System database but are beyond the scope of this book. Hopefully, this assignment will have given you a taste of what relational databases can do. Finally, once a database has been designed and created, the work of the database designer isn't finished. As the system supported by the database develops and evolves the database must be modified to reflect the changes in the system. Good databases are databases that are always up to date.

SECTION 5

Project Guidelines and Sample Exams

How to approach a data base project

Sample Exams

Glossary

How to Approach a Database Project

Database project guidelines

As part of the FETAC (NCVA) Level 2 Database Methods Module you are required to complete a database project. The project tests if you can apply what you have learned about databases to a fictitious problem and then design and create a database to solve the problem. The problem may be in a business context, such as the need to computerise the stock control system of a small business, or it may be in relation to an interest or hobby such as the need to create a database to manage the administration of membership in a local club.

The database project must be completed in three distinct phases.

Phase 1: Design (40%)
Phase 2: Implementation (40%)
Phase 3: Proposed Modifications (20%)

The project must be completed in this order. You must design your database on paper before you set it up in Access. It is worth noting that there are more marks for designing your database and for suggesting modifications than for creating the database in Access. Many students spend too much time on the setting up of the database in Access and not enough time on design and modifications.

Phase 1 – Design (40%)

1. Describe the aims of your project
2. Specify table structure
3. Design a data capture form
4. Specify queries and reports

Describe the aims of your project

1. Provide some background information to set the scene for your project.

Example

Riverstown Karate Club was established in 1998. Since the club was formed, all information about the club and its members has been kept in a paper-based filing system. This is very cumbersome and takes up valuable space. Mistakes have been made from time to time when locating and retrieving information. Not only does it take time to find a member's application form or progress sheet, but it is difficult and time consuming to keep records up to date. The aim of this project is to create a database to store the information relevant to the running of the club. The database will reduce the amount of time necessary for administration work and make it easier for the instructors to run the club.

2. Identify problems that exist in the system you have decided to computerise using a database. For each problem that you identify, describe in detail how the database will solve the problem.

Example

Problem

Gradings occur twice yearly. To prepare for the gradings the instructors draw up lists of members in each belt ranking category. This is very time consuming and sometimes members are unintentionally omitted from the lists. Producing lists of members in alphabetical order is very difficult because the lists are created using a word processing package. If new members join the club prior to a grading, these have to be added to the list of members to be graded by inserting their names in separate word processing documents.

Solution

In the database system, a report will be created to group members according to their current belt ranking. Within each group, members will be sorted in alphabetical order of surname. A report function will count the number of members in each belt ranking category so the instructors know exactly how many students to expect at each grading. If new members join prior to the grading, they will be picked up automatically by the report once they have been entered in the database.

Specify table structure

1. Identify where the data that is going to be stored in your database exists in the current system.

Example

The data relating to members is taken from the club's paper files, i.e. the old system of keeping records. Information on black-belt club members is taken directly from instructors, as is the data on all of the club members due to be graded for their black belt.

2. Specify fields included in the table. For each field, indicate the data type, field size in bytes and give an example of data that will be stored in the field. Identify which field is the primary key.

Example

Membership table

Table 12.1

Field Name	Data Type	Field Size	Example
Membership No	Number	Integer (2)	298
Firstname	Text	12	Richard
Surname	Text	14	Butler
Gender	Text	7	Male
Address1	Text	24	1 Riverstown Wood
Address2	Text	14	Clonmel
Address3	Text	13	Co. Tipperary
Age	Number	Byte (1)	16
Current Belt	Text	10	Yellow
Membership Fee	Currency	8	€360
Date of last fee renewal	Date/Time	8	15/05/2002
Paid	Yes/No	1	Yes

Membership No is the primary key.

Design a data capture form

A data capture form is a printed form used to collect data before it is entered in the database. It should be designed to capture all the input data. We have all filled in data capture forms at one time or another: club membership forms, an application for a bank account or the CAO form. It is a good idea to look at how data capture forms are designed in practice before you create your own data capture form. A well-designed data capture form will

- be easy to complete
- contain instructions on how to complete the form
- indicate whom the form is to be returned to or where the form is to be sent when it is completed

- be well laid out on the page using appropriate fonts, colours, tick boxes and lines (for writing names and addresses).

Specify queries and reports

1. Specify query structure
   The database project must include at least two appropriate queries. At least one query must have an and/or condition. The queries should solve problems identified earlier in the project. Each query should be specified using the following headings:

   - Query name
   - Purpose of query
   - Table(s) linked to
   - Fields in query
   - Query condition(s)

   Example

   Query name: Members eligible for black-belt grading
   Purpose of query: To find all members who currently hold a brown belt and who have paid their membership fee
   Tables linked to: Membership
   Fields in query: Membership No, Firstname, Surname, Age, Current Belt, Paid
   Query conditions:

   Table 12.2

Field Name	Current Belt	Paid
Criteria	"Brown"	"Yes"

2. Specify report structure
   The project must include at least four appropriate reports, two of which must be sorted. (A Mail Merge can be used as a report.) Labels must be produced by one of the reports. The reports should solve problems identified earlier in the project. Each report should be specified using the following headings:

   - Report title
   - Purpose of report
   - Table or query linked to
   - Fields in report
   - Sort and grouping (if any)
   - Report functions (if any)

Example

Report Title: Current Members Belt Rankings
Purpose of Report: This report will display all members' names together with their belt rankings. The report will be grouped by Current Belt.
Linked to: Membership table
Fields in Report: Current Belt, Membership No, First Name, Surname
Sort and Grouping: The report will be grouped by Current Belt and sorted in ascending alphabetical order of Surname within each group.
Report Functions: The function =*count([Membership No])* will be included in the current belt footer to calculate the number of members in each belt ranking category.

Phase 2 – Implementation (40%)

1. Data accurately inputted
2. Database used to sort, query and organise data effectively
3. Reports with headings and sum and average calculation accurately produced
4. Labels with multiple fields accurately produced
5. Database queries and reports saved and printed

Data accurately inputted

Your table should include a minimum of 25 records and 5 fields and must have at least 1 numeric field. Try to include as many different field data types (*Text, Number, Date/Time, Currency, Yes/No, Autonumber, Memo*) as possible in the table – you will learn more from your project as a result. The data should be inputted using a form that is linked to the table. Marks will be deducted for spelling errors. When you have finished inputting the data, proof read it and correct any errors.

Database used to sort, query and organise data effectively

Sorting should be implemented using a report. At least two of the four reports must be either sorted or grouped or both. In the case of the Riverstown Karate Club database, a report displaying members in ascending alphabetical order of Surname could be created. A grouped report could be created splitting members into male and female with a function to calculate the total number of male and female members.

Reports with headings and sum and average calculation accurately produced

The overall formatting of the reports should be attractive and should be consistent across all reports. Data should be aligned under field headings in each report. Headings should be spaced evenly across the page. Sum and Avg must be used in either the report header, report footer or the group footer of at least one report. Other report functions may be used where appropriate. Check the result returned by each function by doing the calculations manually.

Labels with multiple fields accurately produced

In most cases the label wizard is used to create name and address labels. It can also be used to produce labels for other purposes such as price tags and product identification labels. Whatever purpose your labels serve, they will be stored in a report linked to either a table or a query. If you create name and address labels, one of your reports should be a Mail Merge.

Database queries and reports saved and printed

When printing queries and reports, select an appropriate page orientation for each printout. If there are a lot of fields in a particular query or report, set the page orientation to landscape. Reduce paper wastage by checking your queries and reports in print preview and making necessary adjustments before printing.

Phase 3 – Proposed modifications (20%)

Suggest at least three ways in which your database could be improved if you had more time. Students often notice limitations in their database design as they are working on a project. These should be noted and used as potential modifications. Because this section of the project is worth 20 per cent, an in-depth description of each modification is required. Modifications should be illustrated using examples and diagrams where appropriate.

Example

Given more time, there are modifications that would have been quite relevant and useful to include in my project. One such modification relates to the query that finds club members who are under 18. A point to note regarding this query is that a member's age is not constant. As time passes members get older but this is not reflected in the database because their ages are recorded as fixed numbers. So, for example, running the under 18s query today may find 25 members. Running this query exactly one year from now should find less than 25 members because some members will no longer be under 18. In reality, the under 18s query will always find the same number of members unless their ages are updated each year. Because of the way I set up my table, the under 18s query will become more and more inaccurate as time progresses unless each member's age is adjusted on his or her birthday. With more and more members joining the club this method is guaranteed to lead to errors. Given that the main purpose of the database is to reduce the administration work of instructors, this design flaw would be unacceptable in a real-life database.

To solve this problem I would firstly need a date of birth field in the membership table. I would then have to, in some way, calculate a member's age by subtracting date of birth from today's date. In this way the member's age would always be up to date because it would advance with each passing day. This calculation could then be incorporated in the under 18s query so that it always finds only members who are under 18 on a particular date.

Possible database project topics

- **Club membership**
  Create a database to store details of members in a local club. Create queries to find members who qualify for competitions – under 12s, under 15s, under 18s etc. Create a Mail Merge to inform members of club events. Use the label wizard to create a membership card. Create reports detailing competition lists and competition results.
- **Doctor's surgery**
  Store details of patients attending a doctor's surgery in a database. Create queries to analyse how different illnesses occur at particular times of the year. Use reports to calculate the total receipts over a given time period. Create a Mail Merge to inform patients of upcoming appointments and to create reminders for those whose bill is overdue.
- **Technical support**
  Create a database to store details of PCs repaired by technical support. Create queries to analyse the different problems which occur and who fixed them. Create a report to display the number of PCs fixed per week and the average cost of fixing a PC. Create a report that shows which brand of PC gives the most problems.
- **Personal music collection**
  Set up a database to store details of your personal CD or DVD collection. Create queries to find CDs and DVDs by artist, category or title. Create a report which groups CDs and DVDs by category and which calculates the total value of the collection and the average cost of a CD/DVD.
- **Stock control**
  Create a database to store details of stock in a shop or small company. Create queries to find products with low stock levels and products past their sell-by dates. Create reports detailing stock movements, the total value of stock by product and the average stock level.

- **Dating agency**
  Set up a database to store details of a dating agency's clients. Record clients' hobbies and interests and then create queries to match up clients. Use the label wizard to create a membership card. Create a Mail Merge to inform clients of upcoming dates. Analyse weekly and monthly receipts using a report.
- **Car dealership**
  Store details of cars for sale in a database. Create a parameter query that allows customers to specify their preferences (model, engine size, colour) and then finds records matching their requirements. Create a report detailing weekly sales revenue. Create labels that display the registration number, model and colour.

For more ideas, have a look through the examples and database assignments in *Step by Step Databases*.

These are only suggestions. The list of possible database projects is endless. What works best is if you can do your database project on a topic that interests you, e.g. a hobby or an area that you have worked in before.

FETAC (NCVA) Level 2 Database Methods

Sample Exam 1

Michael O'Brien runs a retail outlet in Nenagh, Co. Tipperary. He specialises in a broad range of adhesive and sealing compounds. Recently he has started to record details of the various products which he stocks. Michael wishes to set up a database to record these details and to enable him to retrieve information easily from the data stored.

Task 1

1.1   Create a database named **Stock Control.** Create a table named **Current Stock** to store the data displayed in Table 12.3 on page 231 from the records of Michael O'Brien.

1.2   Complete the database structure form provided (Table 12.6 on page 233) to show field names, data types and field sizes for all fields in the Current Stock table.

Task 2

2.1   Design and create a form to allow the operator to enter the data shown in Table 12.3 in the Current Stock table. The format of the form should be as follows:

- Insert the title **Stock Registration** centrally on the form.
- Display two fields on each line (except the last line).
- Place a label or title beside each field.

Save the form as **Stock registration**.

Print the Stock Registration form (either now or later) **or** call the specialist teacher, **at the end of the examination**, to award marks to your form.

2.2   Input the data shown in Table 12.3 using the Stock Registration form.

Table 12.3

Rec No	Product	Agent	Qty (kg)	Price	Location	Life (wks)
3201	Impact Adhesive	Doyle Bros	5.0	€56.45	Stores	14
3202	Impact Adhesive	Doyle Bros	2.5	€28.50	Shop	12
4215	Sealing Compound	JJ Williams	4.5	€24.80	Stores	28
5247	Roof Sealer	Geo Ryan	5.5	€56.50	Stores	24
5248	Roof Sealer	Geo Ryan	2.5	€28.00	Shop	20
6480	General Adhesive	Geo Ryan	10.0	€120.00	Warehouse	13
6481	General Adhesive	Geo Ryan	5.0	€65.00	Stores	10
6482	General Adhesive	Geo Ryan	2.5	€38.50	Shop	8
7246	Jointing Cement	JJ Williams	25.0	€85.00	Warehouse	6
7247	Jointing Cement	JJ Williams	12.5	€50.00	Stores	5
7248	Jointing Cement	JJ Williams	6.0	€27.50	Stores	4

Task 3

Create queries for each set of criteria listed as follows. **N.B. Print each query as you complete it.**

3.1   Select and print all the records for products which are located in the **shop**. Save this query as **Products in the shop**.

3.2   Select and print all the records for **adhesive** products. Use a wildcard to select the required records. Save this query as **Adhesive products**.

3.3   Select and print all records which are located in the **stores** and where the **qty** (kg) is less than 12. Save this query as **Stock below 12 in stores**.

3.4   Select and print all the records for products where the **agent** is Geo Ryan, where the **price** is between €25 and €90 and the **life** is greater than 12. Save this query as **Geo Ryan**.

Task 4

4.1   Add a new field to the Current Stock table as follows:

> field name – **Toxic**
> field type – **Yes/No**

4.2   Add the Toxic field to the Stock Registration form and enter data as follows:

All the adhesive products are toxic.
All other products are not toxic.

4.3   Delete the record with **rec no** 7247.
4.4   Add the following records using the Stock Registration form:

Table 12.4

Rec No	Product	Agent	Qty (kg)	Price	Location	Life (wks)	Toxic
8324	Quick Adhesive	Doyle Bros	0.5	€6.40	Shop	11	Yes
8325	Bonding Cement	JJ Williams	3.5	€18.60	Stores	9	No

Task 5

5.1   Generate a report from the Current Stock table with the title Current Stock List. Sort the report with the **Product** field in ascending order (primary sort) and the **Life** (wks) field in descending order (secondary sort). Include all fields in the report. Save the report as **Current Stock List**. Print the report (in **landscape** orientation) either now or after the exam has finished. Ensure that data is aligned under each heading and that each text box and label is wide enough to display all data.
5.2   Generate a report from the Current Stock table, to include all the following:

- Show all fields, *except* **Agent** and **Life** (wks).
- Display the appropriate field heading centrally over each column of data.
- Display the title **List of Products**, centrally over the report.
- Sort the report in descending order on the **Price** field.
- Use a function to display the average for the **Qty** (kg) field at the bottom of the report. Insert a label with the text Average Quantity beside the function. Format the average quantity to 1 decimal place.

Save this report as **List of Products**. Print the report (in **portrait orientation**) either now or after the exam has finished.

Task 6

6.1   Produce a set of labels for all products except those located in the warehouse. The labels should have the following format:

- Layout as shown in Table 12.5
- Have more than one label across the page.

Table 12.5

Rec No	Product
Agent	
Price	
Location	

Save these labels as **Stock Control Labels**.

6.2   Print the labels, **Stock Control Labels** (either now or later).

Database structure form

Table 12.6

Field Name	Data Type	Field Size

FETAC (NCVA) Level 2 Database Methods

Sample Exam 2

Paddy Watt's is a bookmaker's chain with outlets in most towns in Ireland. At the Head Office in Galway, a database is required to keep track of bets placed in its various outlets. For this purpose, copies of all dockets are sent electronically to head office. Details are then inserted into the database.

Task 1

1.1   Create a database named **Paddy Watts Betting**. Create a table named **Betting Details** to store sample data extracted from the data received at head office (see Table 12.7).

1.2   Complete the database structure form provided (Table 12.10 on page 236) to show field names, data types and field sizes.

Table 12.7

Docket No	Branch	Received Date	Stake	Payout	Type of Bet
101001	Harbour Road, Arklow	06/08/02	€5.00	€105.00	Treble
101020	Arklow Road, Wicklow	09/08/02	€100.00	€150.00	Single
101067	Shop St, Galway	07/08/02	€20.00	€75.00	Double
101102	Main St, Arklow	06/08/02	€40.00	€120.00	Single
101143	Shop St, Galway	08/08/02	€200.00	€300.00	Single
101147	Shop St, Galway	08/08/02	€500.00	€1,500.00	Single
101154	Bridge St, Waterford	10/08/02	€15.00	€195.00	Yankee
101211	Harbour Road, Arklow	11/08/02	€50.00	€3,000.00	Yankee
101244	Shop St, Galway	13/08/02	€50.00	€400.00	Double
101261	Main St, Arklow	13/08/02	€10.00	€90.00	Single

Task 2

2.1   Design and create a form to allow the operator to enter the data shown in Table 12.7 in the Betting Details Table. The format of the form should be as follows:

- Insert the title **Posting Details** centrally on the form.
- Display two fields on each line.
- Place a label or title beside each field.

Save the form as **Posting Details**.
Print the Posting Details form (either now or later) **or** call the specialist teacher **at the end of the examination** to award marks to your form.
   2.2   Input the data shown in Table 12.7 using the Posting Details form.

Task 3

Create queries for each set of criteria listed below. *N.B. Print each query as you complete it.*

   3.1   Select and print all records for bets at the **Harbour Road, Arklow** branch. Save this query as Harbour Road Arklow.
   3.2   Select and print all records for bets placed in either of the **Arklow** Branches. (Use a wildcard). Save this query as Arklow bets.
   3.3   Select and print all records for bets at the **Shop St, Galway** branch where the **Stake** was greater than €50.00. Save this query as Galway bets above €50.
   3.4   Select and print all records for bets at the Galway or Wicklow **branches**, where the **payout** was between €100.00 and €1,000.00 inclusive and where the **type of bet** was single. Save this query as Single bets in Galway and Wicklow.

Task 4

4.1   Add a new field to the Betting Details table as follows:

field name – **Win**
field type – **Yes/No**

4.2   Add the Win field to the Posting Details form and enter data as follows:

Table 12.8

Docket No	Win
101001	Yes
101020	Yes
101067	No
101102	No
101143	No
101147	No
101154	No
101211	Yes
101244	Yes
101261	No

Task 5

Generate a report, from the Betting Details table (Table 12.7), to include all of the following:

- Show all fields except **Type of Bet**.
- Display the title **Details Posted August 2002** centrally over the data.
- Show a grand total at the end of the report for the **Payout** field.
- Sort in descending order on the **Branch** field (primary sort).
- Sort in ascending order on the **Stake field** (secondary sort).
- Align columns under column headings and space evenly across the page.

Save this report as **Details Posted August 2002**. Print the report (in **portrait orientation**) either now or after the exam has finished.

Task 6

Produce a set of mailing labels for all dockets, *except* those from the Waterford branch. The mailing labels should have the following format:

- Layout as shown in Table 12.9
- Have more than one label across the page
- Print in ascending order by **Branch**.

Save these labels as **Betting Labels**.

Table 12.9

DOCKET NO	RECEIVED DATE
BRANCH	
TYPE OF BET	WIN

Database structure form

Table 12.10

Field Name	Data Type	Field Size

Glossary of Database Terms

Action query

A query that finds records and then either deletes the records, copies them to a new table, appends them onto an existing table or updates them using a formula.

***And* logical operator**

Two or more conditions can be joined in a query by placing all conditions in the criteria row of the query design grid. Access interprets the conditions as being joined using *And*. Only records satisfying all conditions will be found.

Autoexec macro

Once a macro is saved as autoexec, it will run automatically each time the database, in which the macro is stored, is opened.

Autonumber data type

A numeric data type where the field values are entered automatically by Access. It is very useful as a primary key field in a table where new records are frequently generated.

Byte number type

A number data type that stores whole numbers between 0 and 255 in a field. The Byte number type requires 1 byte of storage.

Combo box

An expandable list that can be placed on a form to assist the database user with data entry. Rather than typing the data, the user selects an item from the combo box list. In a single table database, the items in the list are static. In a relational database the items in the list can be static or can adjust as records are added or removed from the database.

Command button

A button that can be placed on a form. Command buttons can be linked to macros. Clicking the command button runs the macro. Command buttons are frequently used to create custom database menus.

Crosstab query

A query that produces a summary based on data that is repeated in two or more fields. The output of the query is arranged, like a spreadsheet, in rows and columns.

Currency data type

A data type used to store monetary values in a field. It is accurate up to 4 places of decimals. The currency data type requires 8 bytes of storage.

Data type

The data type of a field should match the type of data that field will store. Field data types are specified in table design. The main data types are text, memo, number, date/time, currency, autonumber and yes/no. Setting the data type of a field to OLE Object allows you to store objects such as digital images in a field.

Database

A database stores data in a specific structure and order. A database is not necessarily computerised. The Telephone Directory is the most common example of a database.

Database window

The database window displays a list of all objects in the database and divides them into the following categories: Tables, Queries, Forms, Reports, Pages, Macros and Modules.

Date/Time data type

A data type used to store dates or times in a field. A range of formats are allowed. The Date/Time data type requires 8 bytes of storage.

Detail section

The main section of a form. Text boxes linked to table fields are normally displayed in the detail section.

Field

The smallest unit of data in a database. Each record stored in a table is divided into sections, referred to as fields. Fields must be specified in table design before you can enter data in the database.

Field list

The list of fields that can be included in a form or report. If the form or report is linked to a table, all fields, from that table only, can be included in the form. Fields from multiple tables can be included in a form/report by joining tables in a query and then linking the form/report to that query.

Field size

The amount of disk space, measured in bytes, required to store data entered in a field.

Form

An object, whose main function is to facilitate data entry. Controls, such as combo boxes and list boxes, can be used in a form to make data entry quicker and more accurate. Forms can also be used to display records found by a query and as menus in a custom menu system.

Form footer

The bottom section of the form. The form footer normally contains the date or summary information.

Form header

The top section of the form. It normally contains the form title but may also include fields and text boxes containing formulas or functions.

Integer number type

A number data type that stores whole numbers between –32,768 and 32,767 in a field. The integer number type requires 2 bytes of storage.

Label

A label can be used in a form or report to display descriptive text. In a report, labels contain the report title and column or row headings. Fields contained in a form normally consist of a label and a text box. The label is initially the field name but can be edited, as labels do not provide a link to fields in a table. The form title is also contained in a label.

Label wizard

Not to be confused with labels used in forms or reports. The label wizard helps us to create address labels, product labels or any other type of label. The output of the label wizard is printed on special sheets containing sticky labels.

List box

A list that can be placed on a form to assist the database user with data entry. Rather than typing the data, the user selects an item from the list. In a single table database, the items in the list are static. In a relational database, the items in the list can be static or can adjust as records are added or removed from the database. With a list box, all the items in the list are visible so it is not suitable for lists containing a large number of items.

Logical operator

Logical operators can be combined with numbers or text to create query conditions. The query will only display records matching the conditions. The most common logical operators are <, >, and =.

Long integer number type

A number data type that stores whole numbers between –2,147,483,648 and 2,147,483,647 in a field. The long integer number type requires 4 bytes of storage.

Macro

A database object that stores commands in a particular sequence. Running the macro causes all the commands to be executed in quick succession. Macros can be run from the database window or can be linked to command buttons on forms.

Mail Merge

A facility that connects data stored in a table or query with a document created in a word processing package. By placing fields from the table or query in a word processing document, a personalised document can be produced for every record in the table or query.

Memo data type

A data type that can be used to store long text descriptions. The text data type allows a maximum of 255 characters. For field entries longer than 255 characters, the memo data type should be used.

Number data type

If a number will be used in calculations or in conditions that include logical operators it should be stored in a field whose data type is Number. The Number data type should also be used to store numbers which will be sorted in ascending or descending order. A number can be set as Byte, Integer, Long Integer, Single or Double depending on the size of the number and whether decimal places are required.

One-to-Many relationship

When tables are linked in a relational database, the nature of the relationship between the linking fields must be specified. In a one-to-many relationship, the link is between the primary key field on the one side of the relationship and a related field on the many side of the relationship. Data can only occur once on the one side of the relationship, e.g. a customer number, which is the primary key, can only occur once in the Customers table but can occur many times on the many side of the relationship e.g. if a particular customer has ordered 10 products his or her customer number will appear 10 times in the Orders table, but only once in the Customers table.

Or logical operator

Two or more query conditions can be joined in the same field using the *Or* logical operator. For example, in a database that stores data relating to cars, the query condition 'Red' **or** 'Blue' **or** 'Black' would find red, blue and black cars. Conditions entered in different fields can also be joined using the or operator by entering one condition in the criteria row of the query design grid and another condition in the Or row of the query design grid.

Primary key

The field in a table that uniquely identifies each record. Once a field has been set as the primary key, the same data cannot be repeated in that field. In a relational database, the primary key field is used to link tables.

Query

A database object that allows database users to find records matching certain conditions. By entering conditions in the query design grid, database users can specify exactly what type of records they would like to find.

Record

A record contains all the data relating to one item or entity stored in a table. For example, in a table that stores data relating to employees, each record would contain all the data relating to a particular employee. Records are divided into sections, which are called fields.

Referential integrity

A system used by Access to ensure that data in related tables follows certain rules and that data is not accidentally deleted. When referential integrity is enforced you could not, for example, enter an order for a customer in an Orders table unless that customer exists in the Customers table.

Report

The report object allows database users to format, sort and perform calculations on data stored in tables, queries or a combination of tables and/or queries. Data contained in a report can also be grouped into categories with the option of performing calculations on each group.

Report function

Functions, such as Sum, Avg and Count can be included in a report to perform calculations on the data contained in the report. Functions can be included in the report header, report footer, group header or group footer. Functions in the report footer perform calculations on all the data contained in a particular field in the report.

Select query

A query that finds and displays records matching conditions entered in the query design grid.

Single number type

A number data type that stores numbers with up to 7 places of decimals in a field. The Single number type requires 4 bytes of storage.

Tab order

The order in which the cursor moves through text boxes in a form as the tab key is pressed. The tab order should be set up so that the cursor moves from one text box to the next without skipping text boxes. The order should also match the way in which the source data is laid out on a printed page.

Table

A database object that stores data. The table consists of records. Each record is divided into sections, referred to as fields. The table is the most important object in the database. A database cannot function without a table.

Text box

Fields contained in a form or report normally consist of a label and a text box. The text box contains the field name providing the link back to the table or query to which the form or report is linked. Formulas or functions can be entered in text boxes as long as the text box is not bound to a field.

Text data type

The text data type is used to store text and combinations of text and numbers, e.g. a car registration number. The field size of a text field is entered by the database user. Initially it is set to 50 but it should be adjusted to reflect the longest text entry in each text field. The maximum number of characters that can be stored in a text field is 255.

Update query

A query that finds records matching conditions entered in the query design grid and then updates the data in one or more fields by applying a formula. For example, an update query could be used to find all products in a particular category and apply a 10 per cent price increase to those products by multiplying the price field by 1.1.

Wizard

Each time you create a new table, query, form or report a wizard will offer assistance with this task. Most of the wizards in Access are very good and can save you a lot of time by doing the basic set-up of an object for you, giving you more time to work on the finer detail. Within a form or report, the control wizard provides help when objects, such as combo boxes and list boxes, are created.

Yes/No data type

A data type that will only accept one of two values, yes or no, on or off, true or false. Set a field's data type to Yes/No where either yes or no, on or off, true or false is required in a field. For example, in an employee database, the data type of a field named Full Licence could be set to Yes/No. The Yes/No data type requires 1 byte of storage.

144
$$\overset{3\overset{3}{3}8}{\quad}$$
€1,152.00

144
× 2
——
288

144
22×6
——
864

144
$$\overset{5}{2\overset{2}{2}}$$
——
720

「James Joseph O'Mahony

Nora O' Mahony

Miriam Margaret

Ian Anthony

L   James Joseph O'Maho

224 T6F

Rov 24

Row 22 G